CROCK·POT.

◆ THE ORIGINAL SLOW COOKER ◆

3 Books in 1

•5 Ingredients or less

•Chicken

•Soups & Stews

Scalloped Potatoes & Ham
(page 30)

Forty-Clove Chicken
(page 140)

Beggar's Chowder
(page 250)

Publications International, Ltd.

Pictured on the front cover *(left to right):* Scalloped Potatoes & Ham *(page 30)*, Forty-Clove Chicken *(page 140)* and Beggar's Chowder *(page 250)*.

Pictured on the back cover *(left to right):* Easy Dirty Rice *(page 74)* and My Mother's Sausage and Vegetable Soup *(page 242)*.

Introduction

Sizes of CROCK-POT®
Slow Cookers

Smaller **CROCK-POT®** slow cookers—such as 1- to 3½-quart models—are the perfect size for cooking for singles, a couple or empty nesters (and also for serving dips).

While medium-size **CROCK-POT®** slow cookers (those holding somewhere between 3 quarts and 5 quarts) will easily cook enough food at a time to feed a small family. They are also convenient for holiday side dishes or appetizers.

Large **CROCK-POT®** slow cookers are great for large family dinners, holiday entertaining and potluck suppers. A 6- to 7-quart model is ideal if you like to make meals in advance, or have dinner tonight and store leftovers for another day.

Types of CROCK-POT®
Slow Cookers

Current **CROCK-POT®** slow cookers come equipped with many different features and benefits, from auto cook programs to oven-safe stoneware to timed programming. Please visit

www.crock-pot.com to find the **CROCK-POT®** slow cooker that best suits your needs.

How you plan to use a **CROCK-POT®** slow cooker may affect the model you choose to purchase. For everyday cooking, choose a size large enough to serve your family. If you plan to use the **CROCK-POT®** slow cooker primarily for entertaining, choose one of the larger sizes. Basic **CROCK-POT®** slow cookers can hold as little as 16 ounces or as much as 7 quarts. The smallest sizes are great for keeping dips warm on a buffet, while the larger sizes can more readily fit large quantities of food and larger roasts.

Cooking, Stirring and
Food Safety

CROCK-POT® slow cookers are safe to leave unattended. The outer heating base may get hot as it cooks, but it should not pose a fire hazard. The heating element in the heating base functions at a low wattage and is safe for your countertops.

Your **CROCK-POT®** slow cooker should be filled about one-half to three-fourths full for most recipes unless otherwise instructed. Lean meats such as chicken or pork tenderloin will cook faster than meats with more connective tissue and fat such as beef chuck or pork shoulder. Bone-in meats will take longer than boneless cuts. Typical **CROCK-POT®** slow cooker dishes take approximately 7 to 8 hours to reach the simmer point on LOW and about 3 to 4 hours on HIGH. Once the vegetables and meat start to simmer and braise, their flavors will fully blend and meat will become fall-off-the-bone tender.

According to the U.S. Department of Agriculture, all bacteria are killed at a temperature of 165°F. It's important to follow the recommended cooking times and not to open the lid often, especially early in the cooking process when heat is building up inside the unit. If you need to open the lid to check on your food or are adding additional ingredients, remember to allow additional cooking time if necessary to ensure food is cooked through and tender.

Large **CROCK-POT®** slow cookers, the 6- to 7-quart sizes, may benefit from a quick stir halfway through cook time to help distribute heat and promote even cooking. It's usually unnecessary to stir at all, as even ½ cup liquid will help to distribute heat and the stoneware is the perfect medium for holding food at an even temperature throughout the cooking process.

Oven-Safe Stoneware

All **CROCK-POT®** slow cooker removable stoneware inserts may (without their lids) be used safely in ovens at up to 400°F. In addition, all **CROCK-POT®** slow cookers are microwavable without their lids. If you own another slow cooker brand, please refer to your owner's manual for specific stoneware cooking medium tolerances.

Frozen Food

Frozen food can be successfully cooked in a **CROCK-POT®** slow cooker. However, it will require longer cooking time than the same recipe made with fresh food. It is almost always preferable to thaw frozen food prior to placing it in the **CROCK-POT®** slow cooker. Using an instant-read thermometer is recommended to ensure meat is fully cooked through.

Pasta and Rice

If you are converting a recipe for a **CROCK-POT®** slow cooker that calls for uncooked pasta, first cook the pasta on the stovetop just until slightly tender. Then add the pasta to the **CROCK-POT®** slow cooker. If you are converting a recipe for the **CROCK-POT®** slow cooker that calls for cooked rice, stir in raw rice with the other recipe ingredients plus ¼ cup extra liquid per ¼ cup of raw rice.

Beans

Beans must be softened completely before combining with sugar and/ or acidic foods in the **CROCK-POT®** slow cooker. Sugar and acid have a hardening effect on beans and will prevent softening. Fully cooked canned beans may be used as a substitute for dried beans.

Vegetables

Root vegetables often cook more slowly than meat. Cut vegetables accordingly to cook at the same rate as meat—large or small or lean versus marbled—and place near the sides or bottom of the stoneware to facilitate cooking.

Herbs

Fresh herbs add flavor and color when added at the end of the cooking cycle; if added at the beginning, many fresh herbs' flavor will dissipate over long cook times. Ground and/or dried herbs and spices work well in slow cooking and may be added at the beginning of cook time. For dishes with shorter cook times, hearty fresh herbs such as rosemary and thyme hold up well. The flavor power of all herbs and spices can vary greatly depending on their particular strength and shelf life. Use chili powders and garlic powder sparingly, as these can sometimes intensify over the long cook times. Always taste the finished dish and correct seasonings including salt and pepper.

Liquids

It's not necessary to use more than ½ to 1 cup liquid in most instances since juices in meats and vegetables are retained more in slow cooking than in conventional cooking. Excess liquid can be cooked down and concentrated after slow cooking on the stovetop or by removing meat and vegetables from stoneware, stirring in one of the following thickeners and setting the slow cooker to HIGH. Cover; cook on HIGH for approximately 15 minutes or until juices are thickened.

Flour: All-purpose flour is often used to thicken soups or stews. Stir cold water into the flour in a small bowl until smooth. With the **CROCK-POT®** slow cooker on HIGH, whisk the flour mixture into the liquid in the **CROCK-POT®** slow cooker. Cover; cook on HIGH 15 minutes or until the mixture is thickened.

Cornstarch: Cornstarch gives sauces a clear, shiny appearance; it's used most often for sweet dessert sauces and stir-fry sauces. Stir cold water into the cornstarch in a small bowl until the cornstarch dissolves. Quickly stir this mixture into the liquid in the **CROCK-POT®** slow cooker; the sauce will thicken as soon as the liquid simmers. Cornstarch breaks down with too much heat, so never add it at the beginning of the slow cooking process and turn off the heat as soon as the sauce thickens.

Arrowroot: Arrowroot (or arrowroot flour) comes from the root of a tropical plant that is dried and ground to a powder; it produces a thick clear sauce. Those who are allergic to wheat often use it in place of flour. Place arrowroot in a small bowl or cup and stir in cold water until the mixture is smooth. Quickly stir this mixture into the liquid in the **CROCK-POT®** slow cooker. Arrowroot thickens below the boiling point, so it even works well in a **CROCK-POT®** slow cooker on LOW. Too much stirring can break down an arrowroot mixture.

Tapioca: Tapioca is a starchy substance extracted from the root of the cassava plant. Its greatest advantage is that it withstands long cooking, making it an ideal choice for slow cooking. Add it at the beginning of cooking and you'll get a clear thickened sauce in the finished dish. Dishes using tapioca as a thickener are best cooked on the LOW setting; tapioca may become stringy when boiled for a long time.

Milk

Milk, cream and sour cream break down during extended cooking. When possible, add them during the last 15 to 30 minutes of slow cooking, until just heated through. Condensed soups may be substituted for milk and may cook for extended times.

Fish

Fish is delicate and should be stirred into the **CROCK-POT**® slow cooker gently during the last 15 to 30 minutes of cooking time. Cover and cook just until cooked through and serve immediately.

Baked Goods

If you wish to prepare bread, cakes or pudding cakes in a **CROCK-POT**® slow cooker, you may want to purchase a covered, vented metal cake pan accessory for your **CROCK-POT**® slow cooker. You can also use any straight-sided soufflé dish or deep cake pan that will fit into the stoneware of your unit. Baked goods can be prepared directly in the stoneware; however, they can be a little difficult to remove from the insert, so follow the recipe directions carefully.

CROCK-POT® Slow Cooker Recipes with 5 Ingredients or Less

A well-stocked pantry is a shortcut to preparing dishes and entire meals efficiently. The first six chapters of this cookbook take full advantage of the kinds of everyday ingredients most cooks commonly have on hand. They feature recipes that can be created with 5 ingredients and/or the addition of these common pantry items:

- Water
- Milk
- Butter
- Vegetable oil
- Olive oil
- Salt and black pepper
- Other common spices (such as ground cinnamon, ground nutmeg, ground red pepper, red pepper flakes, garlic powder, ground cumin, ground oregano, dried thyme, chili powder, paprika, etc.)
- All-purpose flour
- Cornstarch
- Arrowroot
- Tapioca
- Granulated sugar

These slow-cooked recipes are perfect for busy days when you don't have time to make another stop at the grocery store.

5 Ingredients or Less

TABLE OF CONTENTS

EASY BEEF ENTRÉES...8
Effortless steaks, burgers, stews and more

PORK DISHES 26
Hearty meals made simple with only a few ingredients

CHICKEN & TURKEY 40
Poultry dishes perfect for weekday family meals

ETHNIC RECIPES..54
Travel the globe—in your kitchen—with these exotic flavors

SIDES IN A SNAP 70
Great vegetables and grains to accompany any meal

PIECE OF CAKE..84
Decadent desserts that are unbelievably easy

Easy Beef Entrées

Best-Ever Roast

1 beef chuck shoulder roast (3 to 5 pounds)
1 can (10¾ ounces) condensed cream of mushroom soup, undiluted
1 envelope (1 ounce) dry onion soup mix
4 to 5 medium potatoes, quartered
4 cups baby carrots

1. Place roast in **CROCK-POT®** slow cooker. (If necessary, cut roast in half to fit into **CROCK-POT®** slow cooker.) Combine mushroom soup and onion soup mix in medium bowl. Pour over roast. Cover; cook on LOW 4 hours.

2. Add potatoes and carrots. Cover; cook on LOW 2 hours.

Makes 6 to 8 servings

Veggie Soup with Beef

2 cans (15 ounces each) mixed vegetables
1 pound beef stew meat
1 can (8 ounces) tomato sauce
2 cloves garlic, minced
   Water

Place all ingredients in **CROCK-POT®** slow cooker. Add enough water to fill **CROCK-POT®** slow cooker to within ½ inch of top. Cover; cook on LOW 8 to 10 hours.

Makes 4 servings

Smothered Steak

4 to 6 beef cube steaks (about 1½ to 2 pounds)
   All-purpose flour
1 can (10¾ ounces) condensed cream of mushroom soup, undiluted
1 package (1 ounce) dry onion soup mix
   Hot cooked rice (optional)

1. Dust steaks lightly with flour. Place in **CROCK-POT®** slow cooker. Combine mushroom soup and onion soup mix in medium bowl. Pour over steak.

2. Cover; cook on LOW 6 to 8 hours. Serve over rice, if desired.

Makes 4 servings

Veggie Soup with Beef

Tavern Burger

2 pounds ground beef
½ cup ketchup
¼ cup packed brown sugar
¼ cup prepared yellow mustard
   Hamburger buns

1. Cook beef in medium skillet over medium-high heat until no longer pink, stirring to break up meat. Drain fat. Transfer beef to **CROCK-POT®** slow cooker.

2. Add ketchup, sugar and mustard to **CROCK-POT®** slow cooker; mix well. Cover; cook on LOW 4 to 6 hours. Serve on buns.

Makes 8 servings

Tip: Serve a scoopful on a hamburger bun. This is also known to some people as "BBQ's" or "loose-meat sandwiches." For added flavor, add a can of pork and beans when adding the other ingredients.

Dad's Dill Beef Roast

1 beef chuck roast (3 to 4 pounds)
1 large jar whole dill pickles, undrained

Place beef in **CROCK-POT®** slow cooker. Pour pickles with juice over top of beef. Cover; cook on LOW 8 to 10 hours. Remove beef to platter and shred with two forks.

Makes 6 to 8 servings

Serving Suggestion: Pile this beef onto toasted rolls or buns or, for an easy dinner variation, serve it with mashed potatoes.

Tavern Burger

Easy Beef Stew

2 **pounds beef stew meat, cut into 1-inch cubes**
1 **can (4 ounces) mushrooms**
1 **envelope (1 ounce) dry onion soup mix**
1 **can (10¾ ounces) condensed cream of mushroom soup, undiluted**
⅓ **cup red or white wine**
Hot cooked noodles (optional)

Combine beef, mushrooms, soup mix, soup and wine in **CROCK-POT®** slow cooker. Cover; cook on LOW 8 to 12 hours. Serve over noodles, if desired.

Makes 4 to 6 servings

Tip: Browning the beef before cooking it in the **CROCK-POT®** slow cooker isn't necessary, but helps to enhance the flavor and appearance of the stew. If you have the time, use nonstick cooking spray and brown the meat in a large skillet before placing it in the **CROCK-POT®** slow cooker; follow the recipe as written.

So Simple Supper!

1 **beef chuck shoulder roast (3 to 4 pounds)**
1 **envelope (1 ounce) au jus gravy mix**
1 **envelope (1 ounce) onion soup mix**
1 **envelope (1 ounce) mushroom gravy mix**
3 **cups water**
   Assorted vegetables (potatoes, carrots, onions and celery)

1. Place roast in **CROCK-POT®** slow cooker. Combine soup and gravy mixes and water in large bowl. Pour mixture over roast. Cover; cook on LOW 4 hours.

2. Add vegetables. Cover; cook 4 hours more or until meat and vegetables are tender.

Makes 8 servings

Country-Style Steak

4 **to 6 beef cube steaks**
   All-purpose flour
1 **tablespoon vegetable oil**
1 **envelope (1 ounce) dry onion soup mix**
1 **envelope (1 ounce) brown gravy mix**
   Water

1. Dust steaks with flour. Heat oil in large skillet over medium-low heat. Brown steaks on both sides. Drain fat. Transfer steaks to **CROCK-POT®** slow cooker.

2. Add soup and gravy mixes and enough water to cover meat. Cover; cook on LOW 6 to 8 hours.

Makes 4 to 6 servings

Serving Suggestion: Serve with mashed potatoes.

So Simple Supper!

Swiss Steak Stew

2 to 3 boneless beef top sirloin steaks (about 4 pounds)
2 cans (about 14 ounces each) diced tomatoes, undrained
2 medium green bell peppers, cut into ½-inch strips
2 medium onions, chopped
1 tablespoon seasoned salt
1 teaspoon black pepper

Cut each steak into 3 to 4 pieces; place in **CROCK-POT®** slow cooker. Add tomatoes with juice, bell peppers and onions. Season with salt and pepper. Cover; cook on LOW 8 hours or until meat is tender.

Makes 10 servings

Easy Beef Sandwiches

1 large onion, sliced
1 boneless beef bottom round roast (about 3 to 5 pounds)
1 cup water
1 envelope (1 ounce) au jus gravy mix
   French bread, sliced lengthwise
   Provolone cheese (optional)

1. Place onion slices in bottom of **CROCK-POT®** slow cooker; top with roast. Combine water and gravy mix in small bowl; pour over roast. Cover and cook on LOW 7 to 9 hours.

2. Shred meat using two forks. Serve on French bread, topped with cheese, if desired. Serve cooking liquid on the side for dipping.

Makes 6 to 8 servings

Swiss Steak Stew

Easy Chili

1 teaspoon vegetable oil
1 pound ground beef
1 medium onion, chopped
2 cans (10¾ ounces each) condensed tomato soup, undiluted
1 cup water
Salt and black pepper
Chili powder

1. Heat oil in large skillet over medium-high heat. Add beef and onion. Cook and stir until beef is well browned. Drain excess fat.

2. Place meat mixture, soup and water in **CROCK-POT®** slow cooker. Add salt, pepper and chili powder to taste. Cover; cook on LOW 6 hours.

Makes 4 servings

Tip: This dish can cook up to 8 hours. Garnish with shredded cheese and serve with crackers or thick slices of Italian bread.

French Onion Soup

¼ cup (½ stick) butter

3 pounds yellow onions, sliced

1 tablespoon sugar

2 to 3 tablespoons dry white wine or water (optional)

2 quarts (8 cups) beef broth

8 to 16 slices French bread (optional)

½ cup (2 ounces) shredded Gruyère or Swiss cheese (optional)

1. Melt butter in large skillet over medium to low heat. Add onions; cover and cook just until onions are tender and transparent, but not browned, about 10 minutes.

2. Remove cover. Sprinkle sugar over onions. Cook and stir 8 to 10 minutes or until onions are caramelized. Add onions and any browned bits to **CROCK-POT®** slow cooker. If desired, add wine to pan. Bring to a boil, scraping up any browned bits. Add to **CROCK-POT®** slow cooker. Stir in broth. Cover; cook on LOW 8 hours or on HIGH 6 hours.

3. Preheat broiler. To serve, ladle soup into individual soup bowls. If desired, top each with 1 or 2 bread slices and about 1 tablespoon cheese. Place under broiler until cheese is melted and bubbly.

Makes 8 servings

Variation: Substitute 1 cup dry white wine for 1 cup of the beef broth.

Bacon and Onion Brisket

6 slices bacon, cut crosswise into ½-inch strips
1 flat-cut boneless brisket (about 2½ pounds)
   Salt and black pepper
3 medium onions, sliced
2 cans (10¾ ounces each) condensed beef consommé, undiluted

1. Cook bacon strips in large skillet over medium-high heat about 3 minutes. Do not overcook. Transfer bacon with slotted spoon to **CROCK-POT®** slow cooker.

2. Season brisket with salt and pepper. Return skillet to medium-high heat and sear brisket in hot bacon fat on all sides, turning as it browns. Transfer to **CROCK-POT®** slow cooker.

3. Lower skillet heat to medium. Add sliced onions to skillet. Cook and stir 3 to 5 minutes or until softened. Add to **CROCK-POT®** slow cooker. Pour in consommé. Cover; cook on HIGH 6 to 8 hours or until meat is tender.

4. Transfer brisket to cutting board and let rest 10 minutes. Slice brisket against the grain into thin slices, and arrange on platter. Add salt and pepper, if desired. Spoon bacon, onions and cooking liquid over brisket to serve.

Makes 6 servings

Pork Dishes

Shredded Pork Wraps

- 1 **cup salsa, divided**
- 2 **tablespoons cornstarch**
- 1 **boneless pork loin roast (2 pounds)**
- 6 **(8-inch) flour tortillas**
- 3 **cups broccoli slaw mix**
- ½ **cup (2 ounces) shredded Cheddar cheese (optional)**

1. Combine ¼ cup salsa and cornstarch in small bowl; stir until smooth. Pour mixture into **CROCK-POT®** slow cooker. Top with pork roast. Pour remaining ¾ cup salsa over roast. Cover; cook on LOW 6 to 8 hours.

2. Transfer roast to cutting board. Trim and discard fat from pork. Pull pork into coarse shreds using 2 forks.

3. Divide shredded meat evenly among tortillas. Spoon about 2 tablespoons salsa mixture on top of meat in each tortilla. Top evenly with broccoli slaw and cheese, if desired. Fold bottom edge of tortilla over filling; fold in sides. Roll up completely to enclose filling. Serve remaining salsa mixture as dipping sauce.

Makes 6 servings

Steamed Pork Buns

½ **container (18 ounces) refrigerated shredded cooked pork in barbecue sauce***

1 **tablespoon Asian garlic chili sauce**

1 **container (about 16 ounces) large refrigerated biscuits (8 biscuits)**

Dipping Sauce (recipe follows)

Sliced green onions (optional)

*Look for pork in plain, not smoky, barbecue sauce.

1. Combine pork and chili sauce in medium bowl. Split biscuits in half. Roll or stretch each biscuit half into 4-inch circle. Spoon 1 tablespoon pork onto center of each bottom. Cover with biscuit top, gather edges around filling and press to seal.

2. Generously butter 2-quart baking dish that fits inside **CROCK-POT®** slow cooker. Arrange filled biscuits in single layer, overlapping slightly if necessary. Cover dish with buttered foil, buttered side down.

3. Place small rack in **CROCK-POT®** slow cooker. Add 1 inch hot water (water should not come to top of rack). Place baking dish on rack. Cover; cook on HIGH 2 hours.

4. Meanwhile, prepare Dipping Sauce. Garnish pork buns with green onions, if desired. Serve with Dipping Sauce.

Makes 8 servings

Dipping Sauce: Stir together 2 tablespoons rice vinegar, 2 tablespoons soy sauce, 4 teaspoons sugar and 1 teaspoon toasted sesame oil in a small bowl until sugar is dissolved.

Scalloped Potatoes & Ham

6 large russet potatoes, sliced into ¼-inch rounds
1 ham steak (about 1½ pounds), cut into cubes
1 can (10¾ ounces) condensed cream of mushroom soup, undiluted
1 soup can water
1 cup (4 ounces) shredded Cheddar cheese
   Grill seasoning to taste

1. Spray inside of **CROCK-POT®** slow cooker with nonstick cooking spray. Layer potatoes and ham in **CROCK-POT®** slow cooker.

2. In large mixing bowl, combine soup, water, cheese and seasoning; pour over potatoes and ham.

3. Cover; cook on HIGH about 3½ hours or until potatoes are fork-tender. Turn **CROCK-POT®** slow cooker to LOW and continue cooking about 1 hour or until done.

Makes 5 to 6 servings

Slow-Cooked Pork & Sauerkraut

2 jars (32 ounces each) sauerkraut, drained and rinsed

1 envelope (1 ounce) dry onion soup mix

3 tablespoons brown mustard

2½ cups water

3 pounds boneless pork loin roast

Combine sauerkraut, soup mix, mustard and water in large mixing bowl. Mix well, then add with pork to **CROCK-POT®** slow cooker. Cover; cook on LOW 8 hours.

Makes 6 servings

Easy Pork Chop Dinner

1 large onion, thinly sliced

3 to 4 medium baking potatoes, sliced

6 pork chops

1 can (10¾ ounces) condensed reduced-fat cream of celery soup, undiluted

½ cup water or milk

1. Place onion and potatoes in **CROCK-POT®** slow cooker. Top with pork chops.

2. Combine soup and water in small bowl; pour over chops. Cover; cook on LOW 6 to 8 hours.

Makes 6 servings

Tip: Serve with salad or vegetables for a delicious dinner.

Slow-Cooked Pork & Sauerkraut

Water

1 **boneless pork shoulder roast (3 to 4 pounds)**

   Salt and black pepper to taste

1 **bottle (16 ounces) barbecue sauce**

8 **hamburger buns or sandwich rolls, toasted**

1. Cover bottom of **CROCK-POT®** slow cooker with 1 inch water. Place roast in **CROCK-POT®** slow cooker; season with salt and pepper, if desired. Cover; cook on LOW 8 to 10 hours.

2. Remove roast from **CROCK-POT®** slow cooker; let stand 15 minutes. Discard liquid remaining in **CROCK-POT®** slow cooker. Shred cooked roast using 2 forks.

3. Return meat to **CROCK-POT®** slow cooker. Add barbecue sauce; mix well. Cover and cook on HIGH 30 minutes. Serve barbecue mixture on buns.

Makes 8 to 10 servings

Tip: Depending on the size of your roast, you may not need to use an entire bottle of barbecue sauce. This recipe is equally tasty when made with other cuts of pork roast.

Chorizo Chili

1 **pound ground beef**

8 **ounces raw chorizo sausage, removed from casings**

1 **can (16 ounces) chili beans in chili sauce**

2 **cans (14½ ounces each) zesty chili-style diced tomatoes, undrained**

1. Place beef and chorizo in **CROCK-POT®** slow cooker. Stir to break up well.

2. Stir in beans and tomatoes. Cover; cook on LOW 7 hours. Skim off and discard excess fat before serving.

Makes 6 servings

Serving Suggestion: Top with sour cream or shredded cheese.

Simply Delicious Pork

1½ **pounds boneless pork loin, cut into 6 pieces** *or* **6 boneless pork loin chops**

4 **medium Golden Delicious apples, sliced**

3 **tablespoons packed brown sugar**

1 **teaspoon ground cinnamon**

½ **teaspoon salt**

1. Place pork in **CROCK-POT®** slow cooker; cover with apples.

2. Combine brown sugar, cinnamon and salt in small bowl; sprinkle over apples. Cover; cook on LOW 6 to 8 hours.

Makes 6 servings

Chorizo Chili

Old-Fashioned Split Pea Soup

4 **quarts chicken broth**

2 **pounds dried split peas**

1 **cup chopped ham**

½ **cup chopped onion**

½ **cup chopped celery**

2 **teaspoons salt**

2 **teaspoons black pepper**

1. Place all ingredients in **CROCK-POT®** slow cooker. Stir well to combine. Cover; cook on LOW 8 to 10 hours or on HIGH 4 to 6 hours or until peas are soft.

2. Mix with hand mixer or hand blender on low speed until smooth.

Makes 8 servings

Chicken & Turkey

Creamy Chicken

  3 **boneless, skinless chicken breasts** *or* **6 boneless, skinless chicken thighs**
  2 **cans (10¾ ounces each) condensed cream of chicken soup, undiluted**
  1 **can (14½ ounces) chicken broth**
  1 **can (4 ounces) sliced mushrooms, drained**
  ½ **medium onion, diced**
     Salt and black pepper
     Hot cooked pasta (optional)

Place all ingredients except salt and pepper in **CROCK-POT®** slow cooker. Cover and cook on LOW 6 to 8 hours. Season to taste with salt and pepper. Serve over pasta, if desired.

Makes 3 servings

Tip: If desired, you may add 8 ounces of cubed pasteurized processed cheese spread before serving.

Spicy Turkey with Citrus au Jus

1 **bone-in turkey breast, thawed, rinsed and patted dry (about 4 pounds)**

4 **tablespoons (½ stick) butter, at room temperature**

Grated peel of 1 medium lemon

1 **teaspoon chili powder**

¼ to ½ teaspoon black pepper

⅛ to ¼ teaspoon red pepper flakes

1 **tablespoon lemon juice**

Salt and black pepper

1. Coat **CROCK-POT®** slow cooker with nonstick cooking spray. Add turkey breast.

2. Mix butter, lemon peel, chili powder, black pepper and pepper flakes in small bowl until well blended. Spread mixture over top and sides of turkey. Cover; cook on LOW 4 to 5 hours or on HIGH 2½ to 3 hours or until meat thermometer reaches 165°F and juices run clear. Do not overcook.

3. Transfer turkey to large cutting board. Let stand 10 minutes before slicing. Turn **CROCK-POT®** slow cooker to LOW.

4. Stir lemon juice into cooking liquid. Pour mixture through fine-mesh sieve; discard solids in sieve. Let mixture stand 5 minutes. Skim and discard excess fat. Add salt and pepper, if desired. Return au jus mixture to **CROCK-POT®** slow cooker. Cover to keep warm. Serve au jus with turkey.

Makes 6 to 8 servings

Slow Cooker Chicken and Dressing

4 boneless, skinless chicken breasts
Salt and black pepper
4 slices Swiss cheese
1 can (14½ ounces) chicken broth
2 cans (10¾ ounces each) condensed cream of chicken, celery or mushroom soup, undiluted
3 cups packaged stuffing mix
½ cup (1 stick) butter, melted

1. Place chicken in **CROCK-POT®** slow cooker. Season with salt and pepper.

2. Top each breast with cheese slice. Add broth and soup. Sprinkle stuffing mix over top; pour melted butter over all. Cover; cook on LOW 6 to 8 hours or on HIGH 3 to 4 hours.

Makes 4 servings

Slow Cooker Chicken Dinner

4 boneless, skinless chicken breasts
1 can (10¾ ounces) condensed cream of chicken soup, undiluted
⅓ cup milk
1 package (6 ounces) stuffing mix
1⅔ cups water

Place chicken in **CROCK-POT®** slow cooker. Combine soup and milk in small bowl; mix well. Pour soup mixture over chicken. Combine stuffing mix and water. Spoon stuffing over chicken. Cover; cook on LOW 6 to 8 hours.

Makes 4 servings

Herbed Turkey Breast with Orange Sauce

1 **large onion, chopped**

3 **cloves garlic, minced**

1 **teaspoon dried rosemary**

½ **teaspoon black pepper**

1 **boneless, skinless turkey breast (3 pounds)**

1½ **cups orange juice**

1. Place onion in **CROCK-POT®** slow cooker. Combine garlic, rosemary and pepper in small bowl; set aside. Cut slices about three-fourths of the way through turkey at 2-inch intervals. Rub garlic mixture between slices.

2. Place turkey, cut side up, in **CROCK-POT®** slow cooker. Pour orange juice over turkey. Cover; cook on LOW 7 to 8 hours.

3. Serve sauce from **CROCK-POT®** slow cooker with sliced turkey.

Makes 6 servings

Chicken Sausage Pilaf

1 pound chicken or turkey sausage, casings removed

1 cup uncooked rice and vermicelli pasta mix

4 cups chicken broth

2 stalks celery, diced

¼ cup slivered almonds

Salt and black pepper

1. Brown sausage in large skillet over medium-high heat, stirring to break up meat. Drain fat. Add rice and pasta mix to skillet. Cook and stir 1 minute.

2. Place mixture in **CROCK-POT®** slow cooker. Add broth, celery, almonds, salt and pepper to **CROCK-POT®** slow cooker; mix well.

3. Cover; cook on LOW 7 to 10 hours or on HIGH 3 to 4 hours or until rice is tender.

Makes 4 servings

Cheesy Slow Cooker Chicken

6 **boneless, skinless chicken breasts (about 1½ pounds)**
   Salt and black pepper
   Garlic powder
2 **cans (10¾ ounces each) condensed cream of chicken soup, undiluted**
1 **can (10¾ ounces) condensed Cheddar cheese soup, undiluted**
   Chopped fresh parsley (optional)

1. Place 3 chicken breasts in **CROCK-POT®** slow cooker. Sprinkle with salt, pepper and garlic powder. Repeat with remaining 3 breasts and seasonings.

2. Combine soups in medium bowl; pour over chicken. Cover; cook on LOW 6 to 8 hours or until chicken is tender. Garnish with parsley, if desired.

Makes 6 servings

Serving Suggestion: The sauce is wonderful over pasta, rice or mashed potatoes.

Heidi's Chicken Supreme

1 can (10¾ ounces) condensed cream of chicken soup, undiluted

1 envelope (1 ounce) dry onion soup mix

6 boneless, skinless chicken breasts (about 1½ pounds)

½ cup imitation bacon bits or ½ pound bacon, crisp-cooked and crumbled

1 container (16 ounces) reduced-fat sour cream

1. Spray **CROCK-POT®** slow cooker with nonstick cooking spray. Combine soup and soup mix in medium bowl; mix well. Layer chicken breasts and soup mixture in **CROCK-POT®** slow cooker. Sprinkle with bacon.

2. Cover; cook on HIGH 4 hours or on LOW 8 hours.

3. During last hour of cooking, stir in sour cream.

Makes 6 servings

Tip: Condensed cream of mushroom soup or condensed cream of celery soup can be substituted for cream of chicken soup.

Spicy Shredded Chicken

6 boneless, skinless chicken breasts (about 1½ pounds)
1 jar (16 ounces) salsa

Place chicken in **CROCK-POT®** slow cooker. Pour salsa over chicken. Cover; cook on LOW 6 to 8 hours or until chicken is tender and no longer pink in center. Shred chicken with 2 forks before serving.

Makes 6 servings

Serving Suggestion: Serve on warm flour tortillas with taco fixings.

Ethnic Recipes

Chili Verde

1 **tablespoon vegetable oil**
1 **to 2 pounds boneless pork chops**
   Sliced carrots (enough to cover bottom of CROCK-POT® slow cooker)
1 **jar (24 ounces) mild salsa verde**
   Chopped onion (optional)

1. Heat oil in large skillet over medium-low heat. Brown pork on both sides. Drain excess fat.

2. Place carrot slices in bottom of **CROCK-POT®** slow cooker. Place pork on top of carrots. Pour salsa over chops. Add onion, if desired. Cover; cook on HIGH 6 to 8 hours.

Makes 4 to 8 servings

Serving Suggestion: If desired, shred the pork and serve it with tortillas.

Corned Beef and Cabbage

1 **head cabbage (1½ pounds), cut into 6 wedges**

1 **bag (4 ounces) baby carrots**

1 **corned beef (3 pounds) with seasoning packet***

1 **quart (4 cups) water**

⅓ **cup prepared mustard**

⅓ **cup honey**

*If seasoning packet is not perforated, poke several small holes with tip of paring knife.

1. Place cabbage in **CROCK-POT®** slow cooker; top with carrots. Place seasoning packet on top of vegetables. Place corned beef, fat side up, over seasoning packet and vegetables. Add water. Cover; cook on LOW 10 hours.

2. Combine mustard and honey in small bowl.

3. Discard seasoning packet. Slice beef and serve with vegetables and mustard sauce.

Makes 6 servings

Carne Rellenos

1 **can (4 ounces) whole green chiles, drained**
4 **ounces cream cheese, softened**
1 **flank steak (about 2 pounds)**
1½ **cups salsa verde**

1. Slit whole chiles open on one side with sharp knife; stuff with cream cheese.

2. Open steak flat on sheet of waxed paper; score steak and turn over. Lay stuffed chiles across unscored side of steak. Roll up and tie with kitchen string.

3. Place steak in **CROCK-POT®** slow cooker; pour in salsa. Cover; cook on LOW 6 to 8 hours or on HIGH 3 to 4 hours or until done.

4. Remove steak and cut into 6 pieces. Serve with sauce.

Makes 6 servings

Super-Easy Beef Burritos

1 **boneless beef chuck roast (2 to 3 pounds)**
1 **can (28 ounces) enchilada sauce**
  Water (optional)
4 **(8-inch) flour tortillas**

1. Place roast in **CROCK-POT®** slow cooker; cover with enchilada sauce. Add 2 to 3 tablespoons water, if desired.

2. Cover; cook on LOW 6 to 8 hours or until beef begins to fall apart. Shred beef; serve in tortillas.

Makes 4 servings

Serving Suggestion: Excellent garnishes include shredded cheese, sour cream, salsa, lettuce and tomatoes.

Easy Beef Stroganoff

3 **cans (10¾ ounces each) condensed cream of mushroom soup, undiluted**
1 **cup sour cream**
½ **cup water**
1 **envelope (1 ounce) dry onion soup mix**
2 **pounds beef stew meat**

Combine soup, sour cream, water and onion soup mix in **CROCK-POT®** slow cooker. Add beef; stir until well coated. Cover; cook on LOW 6 hours or on HIGH 3 hours.

Makes 4 to 6 servings

Serving Suggestion: Serve this beef over hot cooked wild rice or noodles along with a salad and grilled bread.

Super-Easy Beef Burritos

Asian Beef with Broccoli

1½ **pounds boneless chuck steak, about 1½ inches thick, sliced thin***

1 **can (10½ ounces) beef consommé**

½ **cup oyster sauce**

2 **tablespoons cornstarch**

1 **bag (16 ounces) fresh broccoli florets**

Hot cooked rice (optional)

Sesame seeds (optional)

*To make slicing steak easier, place in freezer for 30 minutes before slicing.

1. Place steak in **CROCK-POT®** slow cooker. Pour consommé and oyster sauce over meat. Cover; cook on HIGH 3 hours.

2. Combine cornstarch and 2 tablespoons cooking liquid in a cup. Add to **CROCK-POT®** slow cooker. Stir well to combine. Cover; cook 15 minutes longer or until thickened.

3. Poke holes in broccoli bag with fork. Microwave on HIGH (100%) 3 minutes. Empty bag into **CROCK-POT®** slow cooker. Gently toss beef and broccoli together. Serve over cooked rice and garnish with sesame seeds, if desired.

Makes 4 to 6 servings

Mango Ginger Pork Roast

1 pork shoulder roast (about 4 pounds)

½ to 1 teaspoon ground ginger, or to taste

Salt and black pepper

2 cups mango salsa

2 tablespoons honey

¼ cup apricot preserves

Hot cooked rice (optional)

1. Season roast with ginger, salt and pepper to taste. Transfer to **CROCK-POT®** slow cooker.

2. Combine salsa, honey and preserves. Pour over roast. Cover; cook on LOW 6 to 8 hours. Turn **CROCK-POT®** slow cooker to HIGH and cook 3 to 4 hours longer or until roast is tender. Serve over rice, if desired.

Makes 4 to 6 servings

Sandy's Mexican Chicken

2 to 4 chicken breasts

1 medium onion, sliced

1 can (10¾ ounces) condensed cream of chicken soup, undiluted

1 can (10 ounces) Mexican-style diced tomatoes with green chiles, undrained

1 package (8 ounces) pasteurized process cheese spread, cubed

1. Place chicken, onion, soup, and tomatoes with chiles in **CROCK-POT®** slow cooker. Cover; cook on LOW 6 to 8 hours or on HIGH 4 hours.

2. Break up chicken into pieces. Add cheese spread; cook on HIGH until melted.

Makes 2 to 4 servings

Serving Suggestion: Serve over hot cooked spaghetti.

Hot & Sour Chicken

4 to 6 boneless, skinless chicken breasts (1 to 1½ pounds)
1 cup chicken or vegetable broth
1 envelope (1 ounce) dry hot-and-sour soup mix

Place chicken in **CROCK-POT®** slow cooker. Add broth and soup mix. Cover; cook on LOW 5 to 6 hours. Garnish as desired.

Makes 4 to 6 servings

Serving Suggestion: For a nutritious and colorful variation from traditional steamed white rice, serve this dish over a bed of snow peas and sugar snap peas tossed with diced red bell pepper.

Polska Kielbasa with Beer & Onions

⅓ cup honey mustard
⅓ cup packed dark brown sugar
18 ounces brown ale or beer
2 kielbasa sausages (16 ounces each), cut into 4-inch pieces
2 onions, quartered

Combine honey mustard and brown sugar in **CROCK-POT®** slow cooker. Whisk in ale. Add sausage pieces. Top with onions. Cover; cook on LOW 4 to 5 hours, stirring occasionally.

Makes 6 to 8 servings

Mile-High Enchilada Pie

8 (6-inch) corn tortillas
1 jar (12 ounces) salsa
1 can (15½ ounces) kidney beans, drained and rinsed
1 cup shredded cooked chicken
1 cup (4 ounces) shredded Monterey Jack cheese with jalapeño peppers
   Fresh cilantro and sliced red pepper (optional)

1. Prepare foil handles;* place in **CROCK-POT®** slow cooker. Place 1 tortilla on top of foil handles. Top with small amount of salsa, beans, chicken and cheese. Continue layering in order using remaining ingredients, ending with tortilla and cheese.

2. Cover; cook on LOW 6 to 8 hours or on HIGH 3 to 4 hours. Pull out by foil handles. Garnish with fresh cilantro and sliced red pepper, if desired.

Makes 4 to 6 servings

*To make foil handles, tear off three (18 × 2-inch) strips of heavy foil or use regular foil folded to double thickness. Crisscross foil strips in spoke design and place in **CROCK-POT®** slow cooker to make lifting tortilla stack easier.

Sides in a Snap

Barley with Currants and Pine Nuts

- 1 tablespoon unsalted butter
- 1 small onion, finely chopped
- $\frac{1}{2}$ cup pearl barley
- 2 cups chicken or vegetable broth
- $\frac{1}{2}$ teaspoon salt, or to taste
- $\frac{1}{4}$ teaspoon black pepper
- $\frac{1}{3}$ cup currants
- $\frac{1}{4}$ cup pine nuts

1. Melt butter in small skillet over medium-high heat. Add onion. Cook and stir until lightly browned, about 2 minutes. Transfer to 1½- to 2-quart **CROCK-POT**® slow cooker. Add barley, broth, salt and pepper. Stir in currants. Cover; cook on LOW 3 hours.

2. Stir in pine nuts and serve immediately.

Makes 4 servings

Cheesy Corn and Peppers

2 pounds frozen corn kernels

2 tablespoons butter, cubed

2 poblano chile peppers, chopped *or* 1 large green bell pepper and 1 jalapeño pepper, seeded and finely chopped*

1 teaspoon salt

½ teaspoon ground cumin

¼ teaspoon black pepper

3 ounces cream cheese, cubed

1 cup (4 ounces) shredded sharp Cheddar cheese

Chile peppers can sting and irritate the skin; wear rubber gloves when handling peppers and do not touch eyes. Wash hands after handling.

Coat **CROCK-POT®** slow cooker with nonstick cooking spray. Add all ingredients except cream cheese and Cheddar cheese. Cover. Cook on HIGH 2 hours. Add cheeses; stir to blend. Cover. Cook 15 minutes more or until cheeses melt.

Makes 8 servings

Easy Dirty Rice

½ **pound bulk Italian sausage**

2 **cups water**

1 **cup uncooked long grain rice**

1 **large onion, finely chopped**

1 **large green bell pepper, finely chopped**

½ **cup finely chopped celery**

1½ **teaspoons salt**

½ **teaspoon ground red pepper**

½ **cup chopped fresh parsley (optional)**

1. Brown sausage in skillet 6 to 8 minutes over medium-high heat, stirring to break up meat. Drain fat. Place sausage in **CROCK-POT®** slow cooker.

2. Stir in all remaining ingredients except parsley. Cover; cook on LOW 2 hours. Stir in parsley, if desired.

Makes 4 servings

Parmesan Potato Wedges

2 pounds red potatoes, cut into 1/2-inch wedges

1/4 cup finely chopped yellow onion

1 1/2 teaspoons dried oregano

1/2 teaspoon salt

Black pepper to taste

2 tablespoons butter, cut into 1/8-inch pieces

1/4 cup (1 ounce) grated Parmesan cheese

Layer potatoes, onion, oregano, salt, pepper and butter in **CROCK-POT®** slow cooker. Cover; cook on HIGH 4 hours. Transfer potatoes to serving platter and sprinkle with cheese.

Makes 6 servings

Rustic Garlic Mashed Potatoes

2 pounds baking potatoes, unpeeled and cut into 1/2-inch cubes

1/4 cup water

2 tablespoons butter, cut into 1/8-inch pieces

1 1/4 teaspoons salt

1/2 teaspoon garlic powder

1/4 teaspoon black pepper

1 cup milk

Place all ingredients except milk in **CROCK-POT®** slow cooker; toss to combine. Cover; cook on LOW 7 hours or on HIGH 4 hours. Add milk to potatoes. Mash potatoes with potato masher or electric mixer until smooth.

Makes 5 servings

Parmesan Potato Wedges

Pesto Rice and Beans

1 can (15 ounces) Great Northern beans, rinsed and drained

1 can (14 ounces) chicken or vegetable broth

3/4 cup uncooked long-grain white rice

1 1/2 cups frozen cut green beans, thawed and drained

1/2 cup prepared pesto

Grated Parmesan cheese (optional)

1. Combine Great Northern beans, broth and rice in **CROCK-POT®** slow cooker. Cover; cook on LOW 2 hours.

2. Stir in green beans; cover and cook 1 hour more or until rice and beans are tender.

3. Turn off **CROCK-POT®** slow cooker and remove insert to heatproof surface. Stir in pesto and Parmesan cheese, if desired. Let stand, covered, 5 minutes or until cheese is melted. Serve immediately.

Makes 8 servings

Garden Potato Casserole

1¼ **pounds baking potatoes, unpeeled, sliced**

1 **small green or red bell pepper, thinly sliced**

¼ **cup finely chopped yellow onion**

2 **tablespoons butter, cut into pieces, divided**

½ **teaspoon salt**

½ **teaspoon dried thyme leaves**

  Black pepper to taste

1 **small yellow squash, thinly sliced**

1 **cup (4 ounces) shredded sharp Cheddar cheese**

1. Place potatoes, bell pepper, onion, 1 tablespoon butter, salt, thyme and black pepper in **CROCK-POT®** slow cooker; mix well. Evenly layer squash over potato mixture; add remaining 1 tablespoon butter.

2. Cover; cook on LOW 7 hours or on HIGH 4 hours.

3. Remove potato mixture to serving bowl. Sprinkle with cheese; let stand 2 to 3 minutes or until cheese melts.

Makes 5 servings

Spinach Gorgonzola Cornbread

2 boxes (8½ ounces each) cornbread mix

3 eggs

½ cup cream

1 box (10 ounces) frozen chopped spinach, thawed and drained

1 cup Gorgonzola crumbles

1 teaspoon black pepper

Paprika (optional)

Mix all ingredients except paprika in medium bowl. Spray inside of 1½- to 2½-quart **CROCK-POT®** slow cooker with nonstick cooking spray. Pour batter into **CROCK-POT®** slow cooker; cover and cook 1½ hours on HIGH. Sprinkle top with paprika for more colorful crust, if desired.

Makes 10 to 12 servings

Note: Cook only on HIGH setting for proper crust and texture.

Sweet-Spiced Sweet Potatoes

2 pounds sweet potatoes, peeled and cut into ½-inch pieces

¼ cup packed dark brown sugar

1 teaspoon ground cinnamon

½ teaspoon ground nutmeg

⅛ teaspoon salt

2 tablespoons butter, cut into ⅛-inch pieces

1 teaspoon vanilla

Combine sweet potatoes, brown sugar, cinnamon, nutmeg and salt in **CROCK-POT®** slow cooker; mix well. Cover; cook on LOW 7 hours or on HIGH 4 hours. Add butter and vanilla; gently stir to blend.

Makes 4 servings

Orange-Spice Glazed Carrots

1 **package (32 ounces) baby carrots**

½ **cup packed light brown sugar**

½ **cup orange juice**

3 **tablespoons butter or margarine**

¾ **teaspoon ground cinnamon**

¼ **teaspoon ground nutmeg**

¼ **cup cold water**

2 **tablespoons cornstarch**

1. Combine carrots, brown sugar, orange juice, butter, cinnamon and nutmeg in 1½- to 3-quart **CROCK-POT®** slow cooker. Cover; cook on LOW 3½ to 4 hours or until carrots are crisp-tender.

2. Spoon carrots into serving bowl. Transfer juices to small saucepan. Bring to a boil.

3. Mix water and cornstarch in cup or small bowl until smooth; stir into saucepan. Boil 1 minute or until thickened, stirring constantly. Spoon over carrots.

Makes 6 servings

Piece of Cake

Easy Chocolate Pudding Cake

- 1 **package (6-serving size) instant chocolate pudding and pie filling mix**
- 3 **cups milk**
- 1 **package (18¼ ounces) chocolate fudge cake mix plus ingredients to prepare mix**
  Whipped topping or ice cream (optional)
  Crushed peppermint candies (optional)

1. Spray 4-quart **CROCK-POT**® slow cooker with nonstick cooking spray. Place pudding mix in **CROCK-POT**® slow cooker. Whisk in milk.

2. Prepare cake mix according to package directions. Carefully pour cake mix into **CROCK-POT**® slow cooker. Do not stir. Cover; cook on HIGH 1½ hours or until cake is set. Serve warm with whipped topping or ice cream and crushed peppermint candies, if desired.

Makes about 16 servings

Cinn-Sational Swirl Cake

1 **box (21½ ounces) cinnamon swirl cake mix**

1 **package (4-serving size) instant French vanilla pudding and pie filling mix**

1 **cup sour cream**

1 **cup cinnamon-flavored baking chips**

1 **cup water**

¾ **cup vegetable oil**

Cinnamon ice cream (optional)

1. Coat 2- to 4½-quart **CROCK-POT®** slow cooker with nonstick cooking spray. Set cinnamon swirl mix packet aside. Mix remaining cake mix with French vanilla pudding and pie filling mix. Place in **CROCK-POT®** slow cooker.

2. Add sour cream, cinnamon chips, water and oil; stir well to combine. Batter will be slightly lumpy. Add reserved cinnamon swirl mix, slowly swirling through batter with knife. Cover; cook on LOW 3 to 4 hours or on HIGH 1½ to 1¾ hours or until toothpick inserted into center of cake comes out clean.

3. Serve warm with cinnamon ice cream, if desired.

Makes 10 to 12 servings

Cherry Delight

1   **can (21 ounces) cherry pie filling**
1   **package (18¼ ounces) yellow cake mix**
½   **cup (1 stick) butter, melted**
⅓   **cup chopped walnuts**
    Whipped topping or vanilla ice cream (optional)

Place pie filling in 2- to 4-quart **CROCK-POT®** slow cooker. Mix together cake mix and butter in medium bowl. Spread evenly over cherry filling. Sprinkle walnuts on top. Cover; cook on LOW 3 to 4 hours or on HIGH 1½ to 2 hours. Spoon into serving dishes and serve warm with whipped topping or ice cream, if desired.

Makes 8 to 10 servings

"Peachy Keen" Dessert Treat

1⅓   **cups uncooked old-fashioned oats**
1   **cup granulated sugar**
1   **cup packed light brown sugar**
⅔   **cup buttermilk baking mix**
2   **teaspoons ground cinnamon**
½   **teaspoon ground nutmeg**
2   **pounds fresh peaches (about 8 medium), sliced**

Combine oats, granulated sugar, brown sugar, baking mix, cinnamon and nutmeg in large bowl. Stir in peaches; mix until well blended. Pour mixture into 3½- to 6-quart **CROCK-POT®** slow cooker. Cover and cook on LOW 4 to 6 hours.

Makes 8 to 12 servings

Cherry Delight

Cinnamon-Ginger Poached Pears

3 cups water

1 cup sugar

10 slices fresh ginger

2 whole cinnamon sticks

1 tablespoon candied ginger (optional)

6 Bosc or Anjou pears, peeled and cored

1. Combine water, sugar, ginger, cinnamon and candied ginger, if desired, in 6- to 7-quart **CROCK-POT®** slow cooker. Add pears. Cover; cook on LOW 4 to 6 hours or on HIGH 1½ to 2 hours.

2. Remove pears. Cook syrup, uncovered, 30 minutes or until thickened.

Makes 6 servings

Pumpkin-Cranberry Custard

1 can (30 ounces) pumpkin pie filling

1 can (12 ounces) evaporated milk

1 cup dried cranberries

4 eggs, beaten

1 cup crushed or whole gingersnap cookies (optional)

Whipped cream (optional)

Combine pumpkin pie filling, evaporated milk, cranberries and eggs in 2½- to 4-quart **CROCK-POT®** slow cooker; mix thoroughly. Cover and cook on HIGH 4 to 4½ hours. Serve with crushed or whole gingersnaps and whipped cream, if desired.

Make 4 to 6 servings

Cinnamon-Ginger Poached Pears

Triple Chocolate Fantasy

2 pounds white almond bark, broken into pieces

1 bar (4 ounces) sweetened German chocolate, broken into pieces

1 package (12 ounces) semisweet chocolate chips

3 cups lightly toasted, coarsely chopped pecans

1. Place bark, German chocolate and chocolate chips in 3½- to 6-quart **CROCK-POT®** slow cooker. Cover; cook on HIGH 1 hour. Do not stir.

2. Turn **CROCK-POT®** slow cooker to LOW. Continue cooking 1 hour, stirring every 15 minutes. Stir in nuts.

3. Drop mixture by tablespoonfuls onto baking sheet covered with waxed paper; let cool. Store in tightly covered container.

Makes 36 pieces

Variation: Instead of pecans, add raisins, crushed peppermint candy, candy-coated baking bits, crushed toffee, peanuts or pistachios, chopped gum drops, chopped dried fruit, candied cherries, chopped marshmallows or sweetened coconut.

Streusel Pound Cake

1 **package (16 ounces) pound cake mix, plus ingredients to prepare mix**

¼ **cup packed light brown sugar**

1 **tablespoon all-purpose flour**

¼ **cup chopped nuts**

1 **teaspoon ground cinnamon**

Strawberries, blueberries, raspberries and/or powdered sugar (optional)

Coat inside of 1- to 1½-quart **CROCK-POT®** slow cooker with nonstick cooking spray. Prepare cake mix according to package directions; stir in brown sugar, flour, nuts and cinnamon. Pour batter into **CROCK-POT®** slow cooker. Cover; cook on HIGH 1½ to 1¾ hours or until toothpick inserted into center of cake comes out clean. Serve with berries and powdered sugar, if desired.

Makes 6 to 8 servings

Citrus Chinese Dates with Toasted Hazelnuts

  2 **cups pitted dates**
 ²/₃ **cup boiling water**
 ½ **cup sugar**
     Strips of peel from 1 lemon (yellow part only)
     Whipped cream (optional)
 ¼ **cup hazelnuts, shelled and toasted**

1. Place dates in medium bowl and cover with water. Soak overnight to rehydrate. Drain and transfer dates to 3½- to 6-quart **CROCK-POT®** slow cooker.

2. Add ²/₃ cup boiling water, sugar and lemon peel. Cover; cook on HIGH 3 hours.

3. Remove peel and discard. Place dates in serving dishes. Top with whipped cream, if desired, and sprinkle with toasted hazelnuts.

Makes 4 servings

Cherry Rice Pudding

1½ **cups milk**

1 **cup hot cooked rice**

3 **eggs, beaten**

½ **cup sugar**

¼ **cup dried cherries or cranberries**

½ **teaspoon almond extract**

¼ **teaspoon salt**

1. Combine all ingredients in large bowl. Pour mixture into greased 1½-quart casserole. Cover with foil.

2. Place rack in bottom of 5- to 6-quart **CROCK-POT®** slow cooker and pour in 1 cup water. Place casserole on rack. Cover; cook on LOW 4 to 5 hours.

3. Remove casserole from **CROCK-POT®** slow cooker. Let stand 15 minutes before serving.

Makes 6 servings

Chicken

TABLE OF CONTENTS

SAVORY STARTERS 100
Appealing appetizers for snacking or entertaining

STEWS & CHILIES 118
Hearty soups to warm up cold nights

IMPRESS YOUR GUESTS 136
Fabulous fare that frees you up to join the party

EVERYDAY GOURMET....................................154
Make any day feel like a special occasion

WEEKNIGHT WINNERS 172
Easy to prepare family favorites

Savory Starters

Stuffed Baby Bell Peppers

- 1 **tablespoon extra-virgin olive oil**
- ½ **medium onion, chopped**
- ½ **pound ground chicken**
- ½ **cup cooked white rice**
- 1 **tablespoon dry dill weed**
- 3 **tablespoons fresh parsley, chopped**
- 1 **tablespoon tomato paste, divided**
- 2 **tablespoons lemon juice**
- ⅛ **teaspoon black pepper**
- ½ **teaspoon salt**
- 1 **bag yellow and red baby bell peppers (16 to 18 peppers)**
- ¼ **cup vegetable, chicken or beef broth**

1. Heat oil in medium skillet over medium heat. Add onion and cook, stirring, 2 minutes or until onion is translucent. Add ground meat and cook, stirring, 8 to 10 minutes or until thoroughly browned. Transfer meat to bowl. Mix in rice, dill, parsley, ½ tablespoon tomato paste, lemon juice, pepper and salt. Mix well.

2. Using paring knife, make slit in side of each pepper and run under cold water to remove any small seeds. Spoon 2 to 3 teaspoons meat mixture into each pepper.

3. In **CROCK-POT**® slow cooker, whisk together broth and remaining ½ tablespoon tomato paste. Arrange peppers in broth, slit side up. Cover and cook on LOW 5 hours.

Makes 16 to 18 servings

Asian Barbecue Skewers

2 pounds boneless, skinless chicken thighs

½ cup soy sauce

⅓ cup packed brown sugar

2 tablespoons sesame oil

3 cloves garlic, minced

½ cup thinly sliced green onions

1 tablespoon toasted sesame seeds (optional)

1. Cut each thigh into 4 pieces about 1½ inches thick. Thread chicken onto 7-inch-long wooden skewers, folding thinner pieces, if necessary. Place skewers in **CROCK-POT®** slow cooker, layering as flat as possible.

2. Combine soy sauce, brown sugar, oil and garlic in small bowl. Reserve ⅓ cup sauce; set aside. Pour remaining sauce over skewers. Cover; cook on LOW 2 hours. Turn skewers over and cook 1 hour longer.

3. Transfer skewers to serving platter. Discard cooking liquid. Spoon on reserved sauce and sprinkle with sliced green onions and sesame seeds, if desired.

Makes 4 to 6 servings

Chicken Croustade

2 tablespoons canola oil

1½ pounds boneless, skinless chicken breasts, chopped into ¼-inch pieces
   Salt and black pepper

1 shallot, minced

¼ cup white wine

1 large portobello mushroom cap, chopped into ¼-inch pieces

1 tablespoon fresh thyme

¼ teaspoon sweet paprika

¼ teaspoon cumin

¼ cup chicken broth

1 package (6 shells) puff pastry shells *or* ½ package (1 sheet) puff pastry dough*

1 egg yolk

2 tablespoons cream

3 tablespoons freshly grated Parmesan cheese

   Minced chives, for garnish

If using puff pastry sheets, thaw, then slice each sheet into 9 squares; bake according to package directions.

1. Heat oil in large skillet over medium heat. Season chicken with salt and pepper and add to skillet. Brown chicken about 4 minutes; do not stir. Turn and brown other side. Place chicken in **CROCK-POT®** slow cooker.

2. Return skillet to low heat and add shallot. Cook 1 minute until shallot softens. Add white wine. Stir to scrape up any brown bits. Cook liquid down to 2 tablespoons then add shallot mixture to **CROCK-POT®** slow cooker. Stir in mushroom, thyme, paprika, cumin, broth, salt and pepper; mix well. Cover and cook on LOW 3 hours.

3. With 1 hour left in cooking time, bake pastry shells according to package directions.

4. With 20 minutes left in cooking time, beat egg yolk and cream together. Add 1 tablespoon cooking liquid from chicken, beating constantly. Whisk mixture into **CROCK-POT®** slow cooker. Cook uncovered on LOW remaining 20 minutes. Stir in Parmesan. Serve chicken filling over puff pastry; garnish with chives.

Makes 6 to 9 servings

Angel Wings

1 **can (10¾ ounces) condensed tomato soup, undiluted**
¾ **cup water**
¼ **cup packed brown sugar**
2½ **tablespoons balsamic vinegar**
2 **tablespoons chopped shallots**
10 **chicken wings**

1. Combine soup, water, brown sugar, vinegar and shallots in **CROCK-POT®** slow cooker; mix well.

2. Add chicken wings; stir to coat with sauce. Cover; cook on LOW 5 to 6 hours or until cooked through.

Makes 2 servings

Honey-Glazed Chicken Wings

3 **tablespoons vegetable oil, divided**
3 **pounds chicken wings, tips removed**
1 **cup honey**
½ **cup soy sauce**
1 **clove garlic, minced**
2 **tablespoons tomato paste**
2 **teaspoons water**
1 **teaspoon sugar**
1 **teaspoon black pepper**

1. Heat 1½ tablespoons oil in skillet over medium heat until hot. Brown chicken wings on each side in batches to prevent crowding. Turn each piece as it browns, about 1 to 2 minutes per side. Transfer with slotted spoon to **CROCK-POT®** slow cooker.

2. Combine honey, soy sauce, remaining 1½ tablespoons vegetable oil, and garlic in medium bowl. Whisk in tomato paste, water, sugar and pepper. Pour sauce over chicken. Cover; cook on LOW 6 to 8 hours or on HIGH 3 to 4 hours.

Makes 6 to 8 servings

Chicken and Asiago
Stuffed Mushrooms

- **20 large white mushrooms, stems removed and reserved**
- **3 tablespoons extra-virgin olive oil, divided**
- **¼ cup finely chopped onion**
- **2 garlic cloves, minced**
- **¼ cup Madeira wine**
- **½ pound chicken sausage, removed from the casing or ½ pound ground chicken**
- **1 cup grated Asiago cheese**
- **½ cup Italian seasoned bread crumbs**
- **3 tablespoons chopped fresh parsley**
- **½ teaspoon salt**
- **¼ teaspoon black pepper**

1. Lightly brush mushrooms with 1 tablespoon oil and set aside. Finely chop mushroom stems.

2. Heat remaining 2 tablespoons oil in large nonstick skillet over medium-high heat. Add onion and cook until just beginning to soften, about 1 minute. Add chopped mushroom stems and cook until beginning to brown, 5 to 6 minutes. Stir in garlic and cook 1 minute. Pour in Madeira and cook until evaporated, about 1 minute. Add sausage and cook, stirring, until no longer pink, 3 to 4 minutes. Remove from heat and cool 5 minutes. Stir in cheese, bread crumbs, parsley, salt and pepper.

3. Divide mushroom mixture among mushroom caps, pressing slightly on filling to compress. Place stuffed mushrooms in **CROCK-POT®** slow cooker; cover and cook on HIGH 2 hours or until mushrooms are tender and filling is cooked through.

Makes 4 to 5 servings

Chicken Liver Pâté

1½ **pounds chicken livers, trimmed of fat and membrane**

1 **small onion, thinly sliced**

3 **sprigs fresh thyme**

2 **cloves garlic, peeled and lightly smashed**

¼ **teaspoon salt**

3 **tablespoons cold butter, cut into 4 pieces**

2 **tablespoons heavy cream**

2 **tablespoons sherry**

½ **shallot, minced**

2 **tablespoons fresh parsley, minced**

1 **tablespoon sherry vinegar**

⅛ **teaspoon sugar**

Salt and black pepper

Melba toast crackers or toast points, for serving

1. Rinse chicken livers and pat dry. Place in **CROCK-POT®** slow cooker. Add onion, thyme, garlic and ¼ teaspoon salt. Add 1 tablespoon water, cover and cook on LOW 1½ hours.

2. Remove thyme sprigs and discard. Place chicken liver mixture in food processor and pulse to create coarse paste. Add butter pieces one at a time, pulsing to combine. Add cream and sherry and pulse until combined. Transfer mixture to bowl to serve immediately, or place in a small loaf pan and cover with plastic wrap, pressing wrap directly against surface of pâté. Refrigerate overnight until set.

3. Mix shallot, parsley, vinegar, sugar, salt and pepper and let sit for 2 to 3 minutes. Spread on top of pâté. Serve with Melba crackers or toast points.

Makes 8 to 10 servings

Moroccan Spiced Chicken Wings

¼ **cup orange juice**

3 **tablespoons tomato paste**

2 **teaspoons ground cumin**

1 **teaspoon curry powder**

1 **teaspoon ground turmeric**

½ **teaspoon ground cinnamon**

½ **teaspoon ground ginger**

1 **teaspoon salt**

1 **tablespoon olive oil**

5 **pounds chicken wings, tips removed and split at joint**

In **CROCK-POT®** slow cooker, combine juice, tomato paste, cumin, curry, turmeric, cinnamon, ginger and salt. Heat oil in large nonstick skillet over medium-high heat. Add wings and brown in several batches, about 6 minutes per batch. Transfer wings to **CROCK-POT®** slow cooker. Toss well to coat with sauce. Cover and cook on HIGH 3 to 3½ hours or until tender.

Makes 8 servings

Oriental Chicken Wings

32 **pieces chicken wing drums and flats**

1 **cup chopped red onion**

1 **cup soy sauce**

¾ **cup packed light brown sugar**

¼ **cup dry cooking sherry**

2 **tablespoons chopped fresh ginger**

2 **cloves garlic, minced**

Chopped fresh chives (optional)

1. Preheat broiler. Broil chicken wing pieces about 5 minutes per side; transfer to **CROCK-POT®** slow cooker.

2. Combine onion, soy sauce, brown sugar, sherry, ginger and garlic in large bowl. Add to **CROCK-POT®** slow cooker; stir to blend well.

3. Cover and cook on LOW 5 to 6 hours or on HIGH 2 to 3 hours. Sprinkle with chives, if desired.

Makes 32 appetizers

Moroccan Spiced Chicken Wings

Asian Lettuce Wraps

  2 **teaspoons canola oil**
1½ **pounds chicken breasts or pork butt, chopped into ¼-inch pieces**
  2 **leeks, chopped into ¼-inch pieces (both white and green parts)**
  1 **cup shiitake mushrooms, stems removed and caps chopped into ¼-inch pieces**
  1 **stalk celery, chopped into ¼-inch pieces**
  1 **teaspoon toasted sesame oil***
  1 **tablespoon oyster sauce***
  1 **tablespoon soy sauce**
  ¼ **teaspoon black pepper**
  2 **tablespoons water**
  1 **bag (8 ounces) cole slaw or broccoli slaw mix**
  ½ **red bell pepper, seeded and cut into thin strips**
  ½ **pound shrimp, shelled, deveined and cut into ¼-inch pieces**
  3 **tablespoons salted, dry roasted peanuts, lightly crushed**
 10 **to 15 leaves crisp romaine lettuce**
    Hoisin sauce*

Available in the Asian foods aisle of your local market.

1. Heat canola oil in small skillet over high heat. Add meat; cook and stir 4 to 5 minutes or until lightly browned on all sides. Transfer to **CROCK-POT®** slow cooker. Add leeks, mushrooms and celery. Stir in sesame oil, oyster sauce, soy sauce, pepper and water. Combine cole slaw and red pepper slices. Layer on top of meat mixture. Cover and cook on LOW 4 hours for chicken, 5 hours for pork.

2. With 20 minutes remaining in cooking time, stir in shrimp. When shrimp are cooked through, turn off heat and stir in crushed peanuts.

3. Wash lettuce leaves and pat dry. Remove white ribs. To serve wraps, spread hoisin sauce as desired on lettuce leaf. Spoon 1 to 2 tablespoons chicken mixture into leaf and roll up like a cigar.

Makes 10 to 15 wraps

Cranberry-Barbecue Chicken Wings

3 pounds chicken wings
Salt and black pepper
1 jar (12 ounces) cranberry-orange relish
½ cup barbecue sauce
2 tablespoons quick-cooking tapioca
1 tablespoon prepared mustard

1. Preheat broiler. Cut off chicken wing tips; discard. Cut each wing in half at joint. Place chicken on rack in broiler pan; season with salt and pepper. Broil 4 to 5 inches from heat for 10 to 12 minutes or until browned, turning once. Transfer chicken to **CROCK-POT®** slow cooker.

2. Stir together relish, barbecue sauce, tapioca and mustard in small bowl. Pour over chicken. Cover; cook on LOW 4 to 5 hours.

Makes about 16 appetizer servings or 4 main dish servings

For a meal: Serve one fourth of wings with rice for a main dish.

Asian Chicken "Fondue"

1 **cup shiitake mushrooms, stems removed**

2 **cups chicken broth**

1 **tablespoon teriyaki sauce***

1 **small leek, trimmed and chopped (both white and green parts)**

1 **head baby bok choy, trimmed and roughly chopped**

1 **tablespoon mirin (Japanese rice wine)***

2 **tablespoons oyster sauce***

1 **tablespoon canola oil**

2 **pounds boneless chicken breasts, cut into 1-inch cubes**

Salt and black pepper

1 **cup cubed butternut squash**

1 **can (8 ounces) baby corn, drained**

1 **can (8 ounces) water chestnuts, drained**

1 **tablespoon cornstarch**

2 **tablespoons cold water**

Available in the Asian foods aisle of your local market.

1. In **CROCK-POT®** slow cooker, combine mushrooms, chicken broth, teriyaki sauce, leek, bok choy, mirin and oyster sauce.

2. Heat canola oil in skillet over medium heat. Season chicken with salt and pepper and add to skillet. Cook and stir until chicken is lightly browned on all sides. Transfer chicken to **CROCK-POT®** slow cooker. Add butternut squash. Cook on LOW 4½ to 5 hours.

3. With 20 minutes left in cooking time, add baby corn and water chesnuts. In small bowl, whisk together cornstartch and water to achieve consistency of heavy cream. Stir cornstarch mixture into **CROCK-POT®** slow cooker. Continue to cook, covered on LOW remaining 20 minutes.

4. Serve in **CROCK-POT®** slow cooker, set to WARM using bamboo skewers to spear meat and vegetables.

Makes 6 to 8 servings

Thai Coconut Chicken Meatballs

1 **pound ground chicken**

2 **green onions, chopped (both white and green parts)**

1 **clove garlic, minced**

2 **teaspoons toasted sesame oil**

1 **teaspoon fish sauce***

2 **teaspoons mirin (Japanese rice wine)***

1 **tablespoon canola oil**

½ **cup coconut milk**

¼ **cup chicken broth**

1 **teaspoon Thai red curry paste***

2 **teaspoons brown sugar**

2 **teaspoons lime juice**

1 **tablespoon cornstarch**

2 **tablespoons cold water**

Available in the Asian foods aisle of your local market.

1. In large bowl, combine chicken, green onions, garlic, sesame oil, fish sauce and mirin. Mix well with hands and form into 1½-inch meatballs.

2. Heat canola oil in skillet over medium heat. Add meatballs and cook, stirring until lightly browned. Alternatively, place meatballs on a cookie sheet and spray with cooking spray. Broil in oven until lightly browned.

3. Place meatballs in **CROCK-POT®** slow cooker. Add coconut milk, chicken broth, curry paste and sugar. Cover and cook on HIGH 3½ to 4 hours.

4. Add lime juice and mix well. In small bowl, whisk together cornstarch and cold water, stirring until it has consistency of heavy cream. Add to **CROCK-POT®** slow cooker. Cook, uncovered on HIGH 10 to 15 minutes longer or until sauce is thick enough to coat meatballs.

Makes 12 to 15 meatballs

Stews & Chilies

Black and White Chili

- 1 **pound chicken tenders, cut into ¾-inch pieces**
- 1 **cup coarsely chopped onion**
- 1 **can (about 15 ounces) Great Northern beans, drained**
- 1 **can (about 15 ounces) black beans, drained**
- 1 **can (about 14 ounces) Mexican-style stewed tomatoes, undrained**
- 2 **tablespoons Texas-style chili powder seasoning mix**

1. Spray large skillet with cooking spray; heat over medium heat until hot. Add chicken and onion; cook and stir 5 minutes or until chicken is browned.

2. Combine chicken mixture, beans, tomatoes with juice and chili seasoning in **CROCK-POT®** slow cooker. Cover; cook on LOW 4 to 4½ hours.

Makes 6 servings

Serving Suggestion: For a change of pace, this delicious chili is excellent served over cooked rice or pasta.

Chicken Tortilla Soup

- **1 pound boneless, skinless chicken breasts**
- **2 cans (15 ounces each) diced tomatoes, undrained**
- **1 can (4 ounces) chopped mild green chiles, drained**
- **½ to 1 cup chicken broth, divided**
- **1 yellow onion, diced**
- **2 cloves garlic, minced**
- **1 teaspoon ground cumin**
- **Salt and black pepper, to taste**
- **4 corn tortillas, sliced into ¼-inch strips**
- **2 tablespoons chopped fresh cilantro**
- **½ cup shredded Monterey Jack cheese**
- **1 avocado, peeled, diced and tossed with lime juice to prevent browning**
- **Lime wedges**

1. Place chicken in **CROCK-POT®** slow cooker. Combine tomatoes with juice, chiles, ½ cup broth, onion, garlic and cumin in small bowl. Pour mixture over chicken. Cover; cook on LOW 6 hours or on HIGH 3 hours, or until chicken is tender.

2. Remove chicken from **CROCK-POT®** slow cooker. Shred with 2 forks. Return to cooking liquid. Adjust seasonings, adding salt, pepper and more broth, as desired.

3. Just before serving, add tortillas and cilantro to **CROCK-POT®** slow cooker. Stir to blend. Serve in soup bowls, topping each serving with cheese, avocado and a squeeze of lime juice.

Makes 4 servings

Chinese Chicken Stew

- 1 **pound boneless, skinless chicken thighs, cut into 1-inch pieces**
- 1 **teaspoon Chinese five-spice powder***
- ½ to ¾ **teaspoon red pepper flakes**
- 1 **tablespoon peanut or vegetable oil**
- 1 **large onion, coarsely chopped**
- 1 **package (8 ounces) fresh mushrooms, sliced**
- 2 **cloves garlic, minced**
- 1 **can (about 14 ounces) chicken broth, divided**
- 1 **tablespoon cornstarch**
- 1 **large red bell pepper, cut into ¾-inch pieces**
- 2 **tablespoons soy sauce**
- 2 **large green onions, cut into ½-inch pieces**
- 1 **tablespoon sesame oil**
- 3 **cups hot cooked white rice (optional)**
- ¼ **cup coarsely chopped fresh cilantro (optional)**

Chinese five-spice powder is a blend of cinnamon, cloves, fennel seed, anise and Szechuan peppercorns. It is available in most supermarkets and at Asian grocery stores.

1. Toss chicken with five-spice powder and red pepper flakes in small bowl. Heat peanut oil in large skillet. Add onion and chicken; cook and stir about 5 minutes or until chicken is browned. Add mushrooms and garlic; cook and stir until chicken is no longer pink.

2. Combine ¼ cup broth and cornstarch in small bowl; set aside. Place cooked chicken mixture, remaining broth, bell pepper and soy sauce in **CROCK-POT®** slow cooker. Cover; cook on LOW 3½ hours or until peppers are tender.

3. Stir in cornstarch mixture, green onions and sesame oil. Cook 30 to 45 minutes or until thickened. Ladle into soup bowls; scoop ½ cup rice into each bowl and sprinkle with cilantro, if desired.

Makes 6 servings (about 5 cups)

Greek-Style Chicken Stew

2 **cups sliced mushrooms**

2 **cups cubed peeled eggplant**

1¼ **cups reduced-sodium chicken broth**

¾ **cup coarsely chopped onion**

2 **cloves garlic, minced**

1½ **teaspoons all-purpose flour**

1 **teaspoon dried oregano**

½ **teaspoon dried basil**

½ **teaspoon dried thyme**

6 **skinless chicken breasts, about 2 pounds**

 Additional all-purpose flour

3 **tablespoons dry sherry or reduced-sodium chicken broth**

¼ **teaspoon salt**

¼ **teaspoon black pepper**

1 **can (14 ounces) artichoke hearts, drained**

12 **ounces uncooked wide egg noodles**

1. Combine mushrooms, eggplant, broth, onion, garlic, flour, oregano, basil and thyme in **CROCK-POT®** slow cooker. Cover; cook on HIGH 1 hour.

2. Coat chicken very lightly with flour. Generously spray large nonstick skillet with cooking spray; heat over medium heat until hot. Cook chicken 10 to 15 minutes or until browned on all sides.

3. Remove vegetables to bowl with slotted spoon. Layer chicken in **CROCK-POT®** slow cooker; return vegetables to **CROCK-POT®** slow cooker. Add sherry, salt and pepper. Reduce heat to LOW. Cover; cook 6 to 6½ hours or until chicken is no longer pink in center and vegetables are tender.

4. Stir in artichokes; cover and cook 45 minutes to 1 hour or until heated through. Cook noodles according to package directions. Serve chicken stew over noodles.

Makes 6 servings

Chicken Stew with Herb Dumplings

2 cans (about 14 ounces each) chicken broth, divided

2 cups sliced carrots

1 cup chopped onion

1 large green bell pepper, sliced

$\frac{1}{2}$ cup sliced celery

$\frac{2}{3}$ cup all-purpose flour

1 pound boneless, skinless chicken breasts, cut into 1-inch pieces

1 large potato, unpeeled and cut into 1-inch pieces

6 ounces mushrooms, halved

$\frac{3}{4}$ cup frozen peas

1 teaspoon dried basil

$\frac{3}{4}$ teaspoon dried rosemary

$\frac{1}{4}$ teaspoon dried tarragon

$\frac{3}{4}$ to 1 teaspoon salt

$\frac{1}{4}$ teaspoon black pepper

$\frac{1}{4}$ cup whipping cream

Herb Dumplings

1 cup biscuit baking mix

$\frac{1}{4}$ teaspoon dried basil

$\frac{1}{4}$ teaspoon dried rosemary

$\frac{1}{8}$ teaspoon dried tarragon

$\frac{1}{3}$ cup milk

1. Reserve 1 cup chicken broth. Combine carrots, onion, bell pepper, celery and remaining chicken broth in **CROCK-POT®** slow cooker. Cover; cook on LOW 2 hours.

2. Stir remaining 1 cup broth into flour until smooth. Stir into **CROCK-POT®** slow cooker. Add chicken, potato, mushrooms, peas, 1 teaspoon basil, $\frac{3}{4}$ teaspoon rosemary and $\frac{1}{4}$ teaspoon tarragon to **CROCK-POT®** slow cooker. Cover; cook 4 hours or until vegetables are tender and chicken is tender. Stir in salt, black pepper and cream.

3. Combine baking mix, $\frac{1}{4}$ teaspoon basil, $\frac{1}{4}$ teaspoon rosemary and $\frac{1}{8}$ teaspoon tarragon in small bowl. Stir in milk to form soft dough. Spoon dumpling mixture on top of stew in 4 large spoonfuls. Cook, uncovered, 30 minutes. Cover; cook 30 to 45 minutes or until dumplings are firm and toothpick inserted in center comes out clean. Serve in shallow bowls.

Makes 4 servings

Chipotle Chicken Stew

1 pound boneless, skinless chicken thighs, cut into cubes
1 can (15 ounces) navy beans, drained and rinsed
1 can (15 ounces) black beans, drained and rinsed
1 can (14½ ounces) crushed tomatoes, undrained
1½ cups chicken broth
½ cup orange juice
1 medium onion, diced
1 chipotle pepper in adobo sauce, minced
1 teaspoon salt
1 teaspoon ground cumin
1 bay leaf
Cilantro sprigs (optional)

1. Combine chicken, beans, tomatoes with juice, broth, orange juice, onion, chipotle pepper, salt, cumin and bay leaf in **CROCK-POT®** slow cooker.

2. Cover; cook on LOW 7 to 8 hours or on HIGH 3½ to 4 hours. Remove bay leaf before serving. Garnish with cilantro sprigs, if desired.

Makes 6 servings

Quatro Frijoles con Pollo Cantaro

1 cup pitted black olives, drained

1 pound boneless, skinless chicken breasts, cubed*

1 can (16 ounces) garbanzo beans, drained and rinsed

1 can (16 ounces) Great Northern or navy beans, drained and rinsed

1 can (15 ounces) cannellini beans, drained and rinsed

1 can (16 ounces) red kidney beans, drained and rinsed

1 can (7 ounces) chopped mild green chiles, drained

2 cups chicken stock, plus extra as needed

2 tablespoons canola or olive oil

1 cup minced onions

2 teaspoons minced garlic

1½ teaspoons ground cumin

Hot sauce, to taste

Salt and black pepper, to taste

2 cups crushed corn chips

6 ounces Monterey Jack cheese, grated

*Turkey, pork or beef can be substituted for chicken.

1. Combine olives, chicken, beans, chiles and chicken stock in **CROCK-POT®** slow cooker. Mix well; set aside.

2. Heat oil in large skillet over medium-high heat. Cook onion, garlic and cumin until onions are soft, stirring frequently. Add to chicken mixture. Cover; cook on LOW 4 to 5 hours. Check liquid about halfway through, adding more hot broth as needed.

3. Taste and add hot sauce, salt and pepper. Serve in warm bowls and garnish with corn chips and cheese.

Makes 6 servings

Chicken and Chile Pepper Stew

1 **pound boneless, skinless chicken thighs, cut into ½-inch pieces**
1 **pound small potatoes, cut lengthwise into halves, then crosswise into slices**
1 **cup chopped onion**
2 **poblano chile peppers, seeded and cut into ½-inch pieces***
1 **jalapeño pepper, seeded and finely chopped***
3 **cloves garlic, minced**
3 **cups chicken broth**
1 **can (about 14 ounces) diced tomatoes**
2 **tablespoons chili powder**
1 **teaspoon dried oregano**

Chile peppers can sting and irritate the skin, so wear rubber gloves when handling peppers and do not touch your eyes.

1. Place chicken, potatoes, onion, poblano peppers, jalapeño pepper and garlic in **CROCK-POT®** slow cooker.

2. Stir together broth, tomatoes, chili powder and oregano in large bowl. Pour broth mixture over chicken mixture in **CROCK-POT®** slow cooker; mix well. Cover; cook on LOW 8 to 9 hours.

Makes 6 servings

Chicken and Vegetable Chowder

1 pound boneless, skinless chicken breasts, cut into 1-inch pieces

1 can (about 14 ounces) reduced-sodium chicken broth

1 can (10¾ ounces) condensed cream of potato soup, undiluted

1 package (10 ounces) frozen broccoli florets, thawed

1 cup sliced carrots

1 jar (4½ ounces) sliced mushrooms, drained

½ cup chopped onion

½ cup whole kernel corn

2 cloves garlic, minced

½ teaspoon dried thyme leaves

⅓ cup half-and-half

1. Combine chicken, broth, soup, broccoli, carrots, mushrooms, onion, corn, garlic and thyme in **CROCK-POT®** slow cooker; mix well. Cover; cook on LOW 5 to 6 hours.

2. Stir in half-and-half. Cover; cook on HIGH 15 minutes or until heated through.

Makes 6 servings

Variation: Add ½ cup (2 ounces) shredded Swiss or Cheddar cheese just before serving, stirring over LOW heat until melted.

Chicken and Sweet Potato Stew

4 **boneless, skinless chicken breasts, cut into bite-size pieces**
2 **medium sweet potatoes, peeled and cubed**
2 **medium Yukon Gold potatoes, peeled and cubed**
2 **medium carrots, peeled and cut into ½-inch slices**
1 **can (28 ounces) whole stewed tomatoes**
1 **teaspoon salt**
1 **teaspoon paprika**
1 **teaspoon celery seeds**
½ **teaspoon freshly ground black pepper**
⅛ **teaspoon ground cinnamon**
⅛ **teaspoon ground nutmeg**
1 **cup nonfat, low-sodium chicken broth**
¼ **cup fresh basil, chopped**

1. Combine chicken, potatoes, carrots, tomatoes, salt, paprika, celery seeds, pepper, cinnamon, nutmeg and broth in **CROCK-POT®** slow cooker.

2. Cover; cook on LOW for 6 to 8 hours or on HIGH for 3 to 4 hours.

3. Sprinkle with basil just before serving.

Makes 6 servings

Note: This light stew has an Indian influence and offers excellent flavor without the fat.

Chicken and Black Bean Chili

1 **pound boneless, skinless chicken thighs, cut into 1-inch chunks**

2 **teaspoons chili powder**

2 **teaspoons ground cumin**

3/4 **teaspoon salt**

1 **green bell pepper, diced**

1 **small onion, chopped**

3 **cloves garlic, minced**

1 **can (about 14 ounces) diced tomatoes, undrained**

1 **cup chunky salsa**

1 **can (about 15 ounces) black beans, drained and rinsed**

Optional toppings: sour cream, diced ripe avocado, shredded Cheddar cheese, sliced green onions or chopped cilantro and/or crushed tortilla or corn chips (optional)

1. Combine chicken, chili powder, cumin and salt in **CROCK-POT®** slow cooker; toss to coat.

2. Add bell pepper, onion and garlic; mix well. Stir in tomatoes and salsa. Cover; cook on LOW 5 to 6 hours or on HIGH 2½ to 3 hours or until chicken is tender.

3. Increase heat to HIGH; stir in beans. Cover; cook 5 to 10 minutes or until beans are heated through. Ladle into bowls; serve with desired toppings.

Makes 4 servings

Impress Your Guests

Chicken Tangier

- **2 tablespoons dried oregano**
- **2 teaspoons seasoning salt**
- **2 teaspoons puréed garlic**
- **¼ teaspoon black pepper**
- **3 pounds skinless chicken thighs**
- **8 thin slices lemon**
- **½ cup dry white wine**
- **2 tablespoons olive oil**
- **1 cup pitted prunes**
- **¼ cup currants or raisins**
- **½ cup pitted green olives**
- **2 tablespoons capers**
- **Hot cooked noodles or rice**
- **Chopped fresh parsley or cilantro, to garnish**

1. Stir together oregano, salt, garlic and pepper in small bowl. Rub mixture onto chicken, coating on all sides.

2. Spray inside of **CROCK-POT®** slow cooker with cooking spray and add chicken. Tuck lemon slices between chicken pieces. Pour wine over chicken and sprinkle olive oil on top. Add prunes, currants, olives and capers. Cover and cook on LOW 7 to 8 hours or on HIGH 4 to 5 hours.

3. To serve, spoon over cooked noodles or rice and sprinkle with chopped fresh parsley or cilantro.

Makes 8 servings

Stuffed Chicken Breasts

6 **boneless, skinless chicken breasts**

8 **ounces feta cheese, crumbled**

3 **cups chopped fresh spinach leaves**

⅓ **cup oil-packed sun-dried tomatoes, drained and chopped**

1 **teaspoon minced lemon peel**

1 **teaspoon dried basil, oregano or mint**

½ **teaspoon garlic powder**

Freshly ground black pepper, to taste

1 **can (15 ounces) diced tomatoes, undrained**

½ **cup oil-cured olives***

Hot cooked polenta

*If using pitted olives, add to **CROCK-POT®** *slow cooker in the final hour of cooking.*

1. Place 1 chicken breast between 2 pieces of plastic wrap. Using tenderizer mallet or back of skillet, pound breast until about ¼-inch thick. Repeat with remaining chicken.

2. Combine feta, spinach, sun-dried tomatoes, lemon peel, basil, garlic powder and pepper in medium bowl.

3. Lay pounded chicken, smooth side down, on work surface. Place about 2 tablespoons feta mixture on wide end of breast. Roll tightly. Repeat with remaining chicken.

4. Place rolled chicken, seam side down, in **CROCK-POT®** slow cooker. Top with diced tomatoes with juice and olives. Cover; cook on LOW 5½ to 6 hours or on HIGH 4 hours. Serve with polenta.

Makes 6 servings

Forty-Clove Chicken

    1 **cut-up whole chicken (about 3 pounds)**
       Salt and black pepper
    1 **to 2 tablespoons olive oil**
   ¼ **cup dry white wine**
    2 **tablespoons chopped fresh parsley or 2 teaspoons dried parsley flakes**
    2 **tablespoons dry vermouth**
    2 **teaspoons dried basil**
    1 **teaspoon dried oregano**
       Pinch red pepper flakes
   40 **cloves garlic (about 2 heads), peeled***
    4 **stalks celery, sliced**
       Juice and peel of 1 lemon
       Fresh herbs

*The whole garlic bulb is called a head.

1. Remove skin from chicken. Sprinkle chicken with salt and pepper. Heat oil in large skillet over medium heat. Add chicken; brown on all sides. Remove to platter.

2. Combine wine, parsley, vermouth, basil, oregano and red pepper flakes in large bowl. Add garlic and celery; coat well. Transfer garlic and celery to **CROCK-POT®** slow cooker with slotted spoon. Add chicken to remaining herb mixture; coat well. Place chicken on top of celery mixture in **CROCK-POT®** slow cooker. Sprinkle lemon juice and peel over chicken. Cover; cook on LOW 6 hours.

3. Sprinkle with fresh herbs before serving.

Makes 4 to 6 servings

Easy Cheesy Aruban-Inspired Chicken

  1 **can (14½ ounces) diced tomatoes in sauce**
 ½ **cup chicken broth**
 ¼ **cup ketchup**
  2 **teaspoons yellow mustard**
  1 **teaspoon Worcestershire sauce**
 ¾ **teaspoon hot sauce**
  3 **cloves garlic, crushed**
 ½ **teaspoon salt**
 ¼ **teaspoon pepper**
  1 **large onion, thinly sliced**
  1 **large green bell pepper, seeded, cored and thinly sliced**
 ¼ **cup sliced black olives**
 ¼ **cup raisins**
  1 **tablespoon capers**
  4 **to 6 chicken thighs or 4 boneless, skinless breasts**
1½ **cups (6 ounces) shredded Edam or Gouda cheese**
  2 **tablespoons chopped flat-leaf parsley**
    Hot cooked rice (optional)

1. Coat **CROCK-POT®** slow cooker with nonstick cooking spray. Add tomatoes in sauce, broth, ketchup, mustard, Worcestershire sauce, hot sauce, garlic, salt and pepper. Stir well to combine.

2. Add onion, bell pepper, olives, raisins and capers. Stir well to combine.

3. Add chicken. Spoon sauce mixture over chicken until well coated. Cover; cook on HIGH 3 to 4 hours or until chicken is no longer pink.

4. Turn off **CROCK-POT®** slow cooker and uncover. Sprinkle cheese and parsley over chicken. Cover and let stand 3 to 5 minutes or until cheese is melted. Serve over rice, if desired.

Makes 4 servings

Chicken and Artichoke-Parmesan Dressing

2 cans (14 ounces each) quartered artichoke hearts, drained and coarsely chopped

4 ounces herb-seasoned stuffing

1½ cups frozen seasoning-blend vegetables, thawed*

¾ cup mayonnaise

¾ cup grated Parmesan cheese, divided

1 large egg, beaten

½ teaspoon paprika

½ teaspoon dried oregano

½ teaspoon salt

¼ teaspoon black pepper

6 bone-in chicken breast halves, rinsed and patted dry (about 3½ pounds)

Grated Parmesan cheese (optional)

*Seasoning-blend vegetables are a mixture of chopped bell peppers, onions and celery. If you're unable to find frozen vegetables, use ½ cup of each fresh vegetable.

1. Coat **CROCK-POT®** slow cooker with cooking spray. Combine artichokes, stuffing, vegetables, mayonnaise, all but 1 tablespoon Parmesan and egg in large bowl. Stir gently to blend well. Transfer mixture to **CROCK-POT®** slow cooker.

2. Combine paprika, oregano, salt and pepper in small bowl. Rub evenly onto chicken. Arrange chicken on top artichoke mixture in **CROCK-POT®** slow cooker, overlapping pieces slightly. Cover; cook on HIGH 3 hours.

3. Transfer chicken to serving platter. Cover with foil to keep warm. Stir artichoke mixture in **CROCK-POT®** slow cooker. Sprinkle evenly with remaining 1 tablespoon Parmesan. Cook, uncovered, 20 to 25 minutes, or until thickened. Serve dressing with chicken.

Makes 6 servings

Bistro Chicken in Rich Cream Sauce

4 skinless, bone-in chicken breast halves, rinsed and patted dry (about 3 pounds total)

½ cup dry white wine, divided

1 tablespoon or ½ packet (0.7 ounces) Italian salad dressing and seasoning mix

½ teaspoon dried oregano

1 can (10¾ ounces) condensed cream of chicken soup, undiluted

3 ounces cream cheese, cut into cubes

¼ teaspoon salt

⅛ teaspoon black pepper

2 tablespoons chopped fresh parsley

1. Coat **CROCK-POT®** slow cooker with nonstick cooking spray. Arrange chicken in single layer in bottom, overlapping slightly. Pour ¼ cup wine over chicken. Sprinkle evenly with salad dressing mix and oregano. Cover; cook on LOW 5 to 6 hours or on HIGH 3 hours.

2. Transfer chicken to plate with slotted spoon. Turn **CROCK-POT®** slow cooker to HIGH. Whisk soup, cream cheese, salt and pepper into cooking liquid. (Mixture will be a bit lumpy.) Arrange chicken on top. Cover; cook 15 to 20 minutes longer to heat through.

3. Transfer chicken to shallow pasta bowl. Add remaining ¼ cup wine to sauce and whisk until smooth. To serve, spoon sauce around chicken, and garnish with parsley.

Makes 4 servings

Indian-Style Apricot Chicken

6 **chicken thighs, rinsed and patted dry**

¼ **teaspoon salt**

¼ **teaspoon black pepper**

1 **tablespoon vegetable oil**

1 **large onion, chopped**

2 **cloves garlic, minced**

2 **tablespoons grated fresh ginger**

½ **teaspoon ground cinnamon**

⅛ **teaspoon ground allspice**

1 **can (14½ ounces) diced tomatoes, undrained**

1 **cup chicken broth**

1 **package (8 ounces) dried apricots**

1 **pinch saffron threads (optional)**

Hot basmati rice

2 **tablespoons chopped fresh parsley**

1. Coat **CROCK-POT®** slow cooker with nonstick cooking spray. Season chicken with salt and pepper. Heat oil in large skillet over medium-high heat until hot. Brown chicken on all sides. Transfer to **CROCK-POT®** slow cooker.

2. Add onion to skillet. Cook and stir 3 to 5 minutes or until translucent. Stir in garlic, ginger, cinnamon and allspice. Cook and stir 15 to 30 seconds longer or until mixture is fragrant. Add tomatoes with juice and broth. Cook 2 to 3 minutes or until mixture is heated through. Pour into **CROCK-POT®** slow cooker.

3. Add apricots and saffron, if desired. Cover; cook on LOW 5 to 6 hours or on HIGH 3 to 3½ hours or until chicken is tender. Add salt and pepper, if desired. Serve with basmati rice and garnish with chopped parsley.

Makes 4 to 6 servings

Note: Use skinless chicken thighs, if desired. To skin chicken easily, grasp skin with paper towel and pull away. Repeat with fresh paper towel for each piece of chicken, discarding skins and towels.

Coq au Vin

2 cups frozen pearl onions, thawed

4 slices thick-cut bacon, crisp-cooked and crumbled

1 cup sliced button mushrooms

1 clove garlic, minced

1 teaspoon dried thyme

1/8 teaspoon black pepper

6 boneless, skinless chicken breasts (about 2 pounds)

1/2 cup dry red wine

3/4 cup reduced-sodium chicken broth

1/4 cup tomato paste

3 tablespoons all-purpose flour

Hot cooked egg noodles (optional)

1. Layer onions, bacon, mushrooms, garlic, thyme, pepper, chicken, wine and broth in **CROCK-POT**® slow cooker.

2. Cover; cook on LOW 6 to 8 hours.

3. Remove chicken and vegetables; cover and keep warm. Ladle 1/2 cup cooking liquid into small bowl; cool slightly. Mix reserved liquid, tomato paste and flour until smooth; stir into **CROCK-POT**® slow cooker. Cook; uncovered, on HIGH 15 minutes or until thickened. Serve over hot noodles, if desired.

Makes 6 servings

Cook's Nook: Coq au Vin is a classic French dish that is made with bone-in chicken, salt pork or bacon, brandy, red wine and herbs. The dish originated when farmers needed a way to cook old chickens that could no longer breed. A slow, moist cooking method was needed to tenderize the tough old birds.

Chicken Parmesan with Eggplant

6 **boneless, skinless chicken breasts**

2 **eggs**

2 **teaspoons salt**

2 **teaspoons black pepper**

2 **cups Italian bread crumbs**

½ **cup olive oil**

½ **cup (1 stick) butter**

2 **small eggplants, cut into ¾-inch thick slices**

1½ **cups grated Parmesan cheese, divided**

2½ **cups tomato-basil sauce, divided**

1 **pound sliced or shredded mozzarella cheese**

1. Slice chicken breasts in half lengthwise. Cut each half lengthwise again to get 4 (¾-inch) slices.

2. Combine eggs, salt and pepper in medium bowl. Place bread crumbs in separate bowl or on plate. Dip each chicken piece in egg, then coat in bread crumbs.

3. Heat oil and butter in skillet over medium heat until hot. Brown breaded chicken on all sides, turning as pieces brown. Transfer to paper-towel-lined plate to drain excess oil.

4. Layer eggplant on bottom of **CROCK-POT®** slow cooker. Add ¾ cup Parmesan cheese and 1¼ cups sauce. Arrange chicken on sauce. Add remaining Parmesan cheese and sauce. Top with mozzarella cheese. Cover; cook on LOW 6 hours or on HIGH 2 to 4 hours.

Makes 6 to 8 servings

Greek Chicken and Orzo

2 medium green bell peppers, cut into thin strips

1 cup chopped onion

2 teaspoons extra-virgin olive oil

8 skinless chicken thighs, rinsed and patted dry

1 tablespoon dried oregano

$\frac{1}{2}$ teaspoon dried rosemary

$\frac{1}{2}$ teaspoon garlic powder

$\frac{3}{4}$ teaspoon salt, divided

$\frac{3}{8}$ teaspoon black pepper, divided

8 ounces uncooked dry orzo pasta

Juice and grated peel of 1 medium lemon

$\frac{1}{2}$ cup water

2 ounces crumbled feta cheese (optional)

Chopped fresh parsley (optional)

1. Coat **CROCK-POT®** slow cooker with nonstick cooking spray. Add bell peppers and onion.

2. Heat oil in large skillet over medium-high heat until hot. Brown chicken on both sides. Transfer to **CROCK-POT®** slow cooker, overlapping slightly if necessary. Sprinkle chicken with oregano, rosemary, garlic powder, $\frac{1}{4}$ teaspoon salt and $\frac{1}{8}$ teaspoon black pepper. Cover; cook on LOW 5 to 6 hours or on HIGH 3 hours.

3. Transfer chicken to separate plate. Turn **CROCK-POT®** slow cooker to high. Stir orzo, lemon juice, lemon peel, water and remaining $\frac{1}{2}$ teaspoon salt and $\frac{1}{4}$ teaspoon black pepper into **CROCK-POT®** slow cooker. Top with chicken. Cover; cook on HIGH 30 minutes or until pasta is done. Garnish with feta cheese and parsley, if desired.

Makes 4 servings

Note: To skin chicken easily, grasp skin with paper towel and pull away. Repeat with fresh paper towel for each piece of chicken, discarding skins and towels.

Basque Chicken with Peppers

1 whole chicken (about 4 pounds), cut into 8 pieces

Salt and black pepper

1½ tablespoons olive oil

1 onion, chopped

1 medium green bell pepper, sliced

1 medium yellow bell pepper, sliced

1 medium red bell pepper, sliced

1 package (8 ounces) button or cremini mushrooms, halved

2 large cloves garlic, minced

½ cup Rioja wine

1 can (14½ ounces) stewed tomatoes, drained

3 tablespoons tomato paste

½ cup chicken stock

1 sprig marjoram

1 teaspoon smoked paprika

4 ounces diced prosciutto

1. Rinse chicken and pat dry. Season with salt and pepper. Heat olive oil in large skillet over medium-high heat. Add chicken pieces in batches and brown well on all sides. Transfer chicken to **CROCK-POT®** slow cooker.

2. When all chicken has been browned, reduce heat under skillet and add onion. Cook and stir 3 minutes or until softened. Add bell peppers and mushrooms; cook and stir 3 minutes. Stir in garlic, wine, tomatoes, tomato paste, chicken stock, marjoram and paprika. Season to taste with salt and pepper. Bring to simmer; simmer 3 to 4 minutes. Pour mixture over chicken in **CROCK-POT®** slow cooker. Cover and cook on HIGH 4 hours or until chicken is tender.

3. Remove chicken to deep platter or serving bowl with tongs. Spoon vegetable and sauce over chicken. Sprinkle with prosciutto and serve.

Makes 4 to 6 servingst

Everyday Gourmet

Thai Chicken

2½ **pounds chicken pieces**

  1 **cup hot salsa**

¼ **cup peanut butter**

  2 **tablespoons lime juice**

  1 **tablespoon soy sauce**

  1 **teaspoon minced fresh ginger**

     Cooked white rice, for serving

½ **cup peanuts, chopped**

  2 **tablespoons chopped fresh cilantro**

1. Place chicken in **CROCK-POT®** slow cooker. In a bowl, mix together salsa, peanut butter, lime juice, soy sauce and ginger. Pour over chicken.

2. Cover; cook on LOW 8 to 9 hours or on HIGH 3 to 4 hours or until done.

3. To serve, place chicken over rice, pour sauce over chicken; sprinkle with peanuts and cilantro.

Makes 6 servings

Cerveza Chicken Enchilada Casserole

 2 **cups water**

 1 **stalk celery, chopped**

 1 **small carrot, peeled and chopped**

 1 **bottle (12 ounces) Mexican beer, divided**

   Juice of 1 lime

 1 **teaspoon salt**

1½ **pounds boneless, skinless chicken breasts**

 1 **can (19 ounces) enchilada sauce, divided**

 7 **ounces white corn tortilla chips**

½ **medium onion, chopped**

 3 **cups shredded Cheddar cheese**

   Sour cream, sliced olives and cilantro (optional)

1. Heat water, celery, carrot, 1 cup beer, lime juice and salt in saucepan over high heat until boiling. Add chicken breasts; reduce heat to simmer. Cook until chicken is cooked through, about 12 to 14 minutes. Remove; cool and shred into bite-sized pieces.

2. Spoon ½ cup enchilada sauce in bottom of **CROCK-POT®** slow cooker. Place tortilla chips in 1 layer over sauce. Cover with ⅓ shredded chicken. Sprinkle ⅓ chopped onion over chicken. Add 1 cup cheese, spreading evenly. Pour ½ cup enchilada sauce over cheese. Repeat layering process 2 more times, pouring remaining beer over casserole before adding last layer of cheese.

3. Cook on LOW 3½ to 4 hours. Top with sour cream, sliced olives and cilantro, if desired.

Makes 4 to 6 servings

Mediterranean Chicken Breasts and Wild Rice

  1 **pound boneless, skinless chicken breasts, lightly pounded**
    Kosher salt, to taste
    Black pepper, to taste
  1 **cup white and wild rice blend**
 10 **cloves garlic, smashed**
 ½ **cup oil-packed or dry sun-dried tomatoes***
 ½ **cup capers, drained**
  2 **cups water**
 ½ **cup fresh-squeezed lemon juice**
 ¼ **cup extra-virgin olive oil**

If using dry sun-dried tomatoes, soak in boiling water to soften before chopping.

1. Season chicken with salt and black pepper. Place in **CROCK-POT®** slow cooker. Add rice, garlic, tomatoes and capers; stir well.

2. Mix water, lemon juice and oil in small mixing bowl. Pour mixture over rice and chicken. Stir once to coat chicken. Cover; cook on LOW 8 hours.

Makes 4 servings

Dijon Chicken Thighs with Artichoke Sauce

⅓ **cup Dijon mustard**

2 **tablespoons chopped garlic**

½ **teaspoon dried tarragon**

2½ **pounds chicken thighs (about 8), skinned**

1 **cup chopped onion**

1 **cup sliced mushrooms**

1 **jar (12 ounces) quartered marinated artichoke hearts, undrained**

¼ **cup chopped fresh parsley**

1. Combine mustard, garlic and tarragon in large bowl. Add chicken thighs and toss to coat. Transfer to **CROCK-POT®** slow cooker.

2. Add onion, mushrooms and artichokes with liquid. Cover; cook on LOW 6 to 8 hours or on HIGH 4 hours or until chicken is tender. Stir in parsley just before serving.

Makes 8 servings

Serving Suggestion: Serve with hot fettuccine that has been tossed with butter and parsley.

Note: To skin chicken easily, grasp skin with paper towel and pull away. Repeat with fresh paper towel for each piece of chicken, discarding skins and towels.

Chipotle Chicken Casserole

- 1 **pound boneless, skinless chicken thighs, cut into cubes**
- 1 **teaspoon salt**
- 1 **teaspoon ground cumin**
- 1 **bay leaf**
- 1 **chipotle pepper in adobo sauce, minced**
- 1 **medium onion, diced**
- 1 **can (15 ounces) navy beans, drained and rinsed**
- 1 **can (15 ounces) black beans, drained and rinsed**
- 1 **can (14½ ounces) crushed tomatoes, undrained**
- 1½ **cups chicken broth**
- ½ **cup orange juice**
- ¼ **cup chopped fresh cilantro, for garnish (optional)**

Combine chicken, salt, cumin, bay leaf, chipotle pepper, onion, beans, tomatoes with juice, broth and orange juice in **CROCK-POT®** slow cooker. Cover; cook on LOW 7 to 8 hours or on HIGH 3½ to 4 hours. Remove bay leaf before serving. Garnish with cilantro, if desired.

Makes 6 servings

Autumn Chicken

 1 **can (14 ounces) whole artichoke hearts, drained**
 1 **can (14 ounces) whole mushrooms, divided**
12 **boneless, skinless chicken breasts**
 1 **jar (6½ ounces) marinated artichoke hearts, with liquid**
¾ **cup white wine**
½ **cup balsamic vinaigrette**
    Hot cooked noodles
    Paprika, for garnish (optional)

Spread whole artichokes over bottom of **CROCK-POT®** slow cooker. Top with half the mushrooms. Layer chicken over mushrooms. Add marinated artichoke hearts with liquid. Add remaining mushrooms. Pour in wine and vinaigrette. Cover; cook on LOW 4 to 5 hours. Serve over noodles. Garnish with paprika, if desired.

Makes 10 to 12 servings

Chicken & Rice

 3 **cans (10¾ ounces each) condensed cream of chicken soup, undiluted**
 2 **cups uncooked instant rice**
 1 **cup water**
 1 **pound boneless, skinless chicken breasts or chicken breast tenders**
½ **teaspoon salt**
¼ **teaspoon paprika**
¼ **teaspoon black pepper**
½ **cup diced celery**

Combine soup, rice and water in **CROCK-POT®** slow cooker. Add chicken; sprinkle with salt, paprika and pepper. Sprinkle celery over chicken. Cover; cook on LOW 6 to 8 hours or on HIGH 3 to 4 hours.

Makes 4 servings

Autumn Chicken

Chicken in Honey Sauce

4 to 6 boneless, skinless chicken breasts
Salt
Black pepper
2 cups honey
1 cup soy sauce
½ cup ketchup
¼ cup oil
2 cloves garlic, minced
Sesame seeds

1. Place chicken in **CROCK-POT®** slow cooker; season with salt and pepper.

2. Combine honey, soy sauce, ketchup, oil and garlic in medium bowl. Pour over chicken. Cover; cook on LOW 6 to 8 hours or on HIGH 3 to 4 hours.

3. Garnish with sesame seeds before serving.

Makes 4 to 6 servings

Chicken Teriyaki

1 pound boneless, skinless chicken tenders
1 can (6 ounces) pineapple juice
¼ cup soy sauce
1 tablespoon sugar
1 tablespoon minced fresh ginger
1 tablespoon minced garlic
1 tablespoon vegetable oil
1 tablespoon molasses
24 cherry tomatoes (optional)
2 cups hot cooked rice

Combine all ingredients except rice in **CROCK-POT®** slow cooker. Cover; cook on LOW 2 hours or until chicken is tender. Serve chicken and sauce over rice.

Makes 4 servings

Chicken in Honey Sauce

Provençal Lemon and Olive Chicken

2 **cups chopped onion**

8 **skinless chicken thighs (about 2½ pounds)**

1 **lemon, thinly sliced and seeds removed**

1 **cup pitted green olives**

1 **tablespoon olive brine from jar or 1 tablespoon white vinegar**

2 **teaspoons herbes de Provence**

1 **bay leaf**

½ **teaspoon salt**

⅛ **teaspoon black pepper**

1 **cup chicken broth**

½ **cup minced fresh parsley**

1. Place onion in **CROCK-POT®** slow cooker. Arrange chicken thighs over onion. Place lemon slice on each thigh. Add olives, brine, herbes de Provence, bay leaf, salt and pepper. Slowly pour in chicken broth.

2. Cover; cook on LOW 5 to 6 hours or on HIGH 3 to 3½ hours or until chicken is tender. Stir in parsley before serving.

Makes 8 servings

Note: To skin chicken easily, grasp skin with paper towel and pull away. Repeat with fresh paper towel for each piece of chicken, discarding skins and towels.

Herbed Artichoke Chicken

1½ **pounds boneless, skinless chicken breasts**
1 **can (14 ounces) tomatoes, drained and diced**
1 **can (14 ounces) artichoke hearts in water, drained**
1 **small onion, chopped**
½ **cup kalamata olives, pitted and sliced**
1 **cup fat-free chicken broth**
¼ **cup dry white wine**
3 **tablespoons quick-cooking tapioca**
2 **teaspoons curry powder**
1 **tablespoon chopped fresh Italian parsley**
1 **teaspoon dried sweet basil**
1 **teaspoon dried thyme leaves**
½ **teaspoon salt**
½ **teaspoon freshly ground black pepper**

1. Combine chicken, tomatoes, artichokes, onion, olives, broth, wine, tapioca, curry powder, parsley, basil, thyme, salt and pepper in **CROCK-POT®** slow cooker. Mix thoroughly.

2. Cover; cook on LOW for 6 to 8 hours or on HIGH for 3½ to 4 hours or until chicken is no longer pink in center.

Makes 6 servings

Tip: For a larger crowd, use a 5-, 6- or 7-quart **CROCK-POT®** slow cooker and double all ingredients, except the chicken broth and white wine. Increase the chicken broth and white wine by one half.

Chicken Parisienne

6 boneless, skinless chicken breasts (about 1½ pounds), cubed

½ teaspoon salt

½ teaspoon black pepper

½ teaspoon paprika

1 can (10¾ ounces) condensed cream of mushroom or cream of chicken soup, undiluted

2 cans (4 ounces each) sliced mushrooms, drained

½ cup dry white wine

1 cup sour cream

6 cups hot cooked egg noodles

1. Place chicken in **CROCK-POT®** slow cooker. Sprinkle with salt, pepper and paprika. Add soup, mushrooms and wine to slow cooker; mix well.

2. Cover; cook on HIGH 2 to 3 hours.

3. Stir in sour cream during last 30 minutes of cooking. Serve over noodles. Garnish as desired.

Makes 6 servings

Serving Suggestion: Try this dish over rice instead of noodles.

Cashew Chicken

6 **boneless, skinless chicken breasts**

1½ **cups cashews**

1 **cup sliced mushrooms**

1 **cup sliced celery**

1 **can (10¾ ounces) condensed cream of mushroom soup, undiluted**

¼ **cup chopped green onion**

2 **tablespoons butter**

1½ **tablespoons soy sauce**

Hot cooked rice

1. Combine chicken, cashews, mushrooms, celery, soup, green onion, butter and soy sauce in **CROCK-POT®** slow cooker.

2. Cover; cook on LOW 6 to 8 hours or on HIGH 4 to 6 hours or until done. Serve over rice.

Note: Time spent in the kitchen cooking with your kids is time well spent. You can share the value of preparing wholesome, comforting, nurturing foods while equipping them with the skills to create their own food traditions in the future. Even young children can participate in family meal preparation. Just remember these basics: Always make sure children are well-supervised in the kitchen. Only adults should use sharp utensils, plug in or turn on electric appliances or handle hot foods. Be sure to only assign tasks that the child can do and feel good about.

Makes 6 servings

Weeknight Winners

Spanish Paella with Chicken and Sausage

- 1 **tablespoon olive oil**
- 2 **pounds chicken thighs**
- 1 **medium onion, chopped**
- 1 **clove garlic, minced**
- 1 **pound hot smoked sausages, sliced**
- 1 **can (14½ ounces) stewed tomatoes**
- 1 **cup Arborio rice**
- 4 **cups chicken broth**
- 1 **pinch saffron (optional)**
- ½ **cup frozen peas, thawed**

1. Heat oil in large skillet over medium-high heat. Brown chicken on all sides and place in **CROCK-POT®** slow cooker.

2. Add onions to skillet, cook and stir until translucent. Stir in garlic, sausages, tomatoes, rice, chicken broth and saffron. Pour mixture over chicken.

3. Cover and cook on HIGH 3 to 4 hours or until chicken and rice are tender. Remove chicken pieces to platter and fluff rice with fork. Stir in peas. Spoon rice onto platter with chicken.

Makes 4 servings

Greek Chicken Pitas with Creamy Mustard Sauce

Filling

- 1 **medium green bell pepper, cored, seeded and sliced into ½-inch strips**
- 1 **medium onion, cut into 8 wedges**
- 1 **pound boneless skinless chicken breasts, rinsed and patted dry**
- 1 **tablespoon extra-virgin olive oil**
- 2 **teaspoons dried Greek seasoning blend**
- ¼ **teaspoon salt**

Sauce

- ¼ **cup plain fat-free yogurt**
- ¼ **cup mayonnaise**
- 1 **tablespoon prepared mustard**
- ¼ **teaspoon salt**
- 4 **whole pita rounds**
- ½ **cup crumbled feta cheese**

  Optional toppings: Sliced cucumbers, sliced tomatoes, Kalamata olives

1. Coat **CROCK-POT®** slow cooker with nonstick cooking spray. Place bell pepper and onion in bottom. Add chicken, and drizzle on oil. Sprinkle evenly with seasoning and ¼ teaspoon salt. Cover; cook on HIGH 1¾ hours or until chicken is no longer pink and vegetables are crisp-tender.

2. Remove chicken and slice. Remove vegetables using slotted spoon.

3. To prepare sauce: Combine yogurt, mayonnaise, mustard and ¼ teaspoon salt in small bowl. Whisk until smooth.

4. Warm pitas according to package directions. Cut in half, and fill with chicken, sauce, vegetables and feta cheese. Top as desired.

Makes 4 servings

Roast Chicken with Peas, Prosciutto and Cream

1 cut-up whole chicken (about 2½ pounds)
  Salt and black pepper, to taste
5 ounces prosciutto, diced
1 small white onion, finely chopped
½ cup dry white wine
1 package (10 ounces) frozen peas
½ cup heavy cream
1½ tablespoons cornstarch
2 tablespoons water
4 cups farfalle pasta, cooked al dente

1. Season chicken pieces with salt and pepper. Combine chicken, prosciutto, onion and wine in **CROCK-POT®** slow cooker. Cover; cook on HIGH 3½ to 4 hours or on LOW 8 to 10 hours, until chicken is no longer pink in center.

2. During last 30 minutes of cooking, add frozen peas and heavy cream to cooking liquid.

3. Remove chicken with slotted spoon. Carve meat and set aside on warmed platter.

4. Combine cornstarch and water. Add to cooking liquid in **CROCK-POT®** slow cooker. Cover; cook on HIGH 10 to 15 minutes or until thickened.

5. To serve, spoon pasta onto individual plates. Place chicken on pasta and top each portion with sauce.

Makes 6 servings

Chicken and Ham with Biscuits

2 cans (10¾ ounces each) condensed cream of mushroom soup, undiluted

2 cups diced ham

2 cups diced boneless chicken

1 package (12 ounces) frozen peas and onions

1 package (8 ounces) frozen corn

½ cup chopped celery

¼ teaspoon dried marjoram

¼ teaspoon dried thyme

2 tablespoons cornstarch

2 teaspoons water

1 to 2 cans refrigerated buttermilk biscuits

4 tablespoons (½ stick) butter, melted

1. Combine soup, ham, chicken, frozen vegetables, celery, marjoram and thyme in **CROCK-POT®** slow cooker. Cover; cook on LOW 4 to 5 hours or on HIGH 1 to 3 hours.

2. Mix cornstarch and water together in bowl. Stir into **CROCK-POT®** slow cooker. Cook 10 to 15 minutes longer or until mixture has thickened.

3. Meanwhile, place biscuits on baking sheet and brush with butter. Bake according to package directions until biscuits are golden brown.

4. To serve, ladle stew into bowls and top with warm biscuit.

Makes 8 to 10 servings

Braised Italian Chicken with Tomatoes and Olives

- **2 pounds boneless, skinless chicken thighs**
- **1 teaspoon kosher salt**
- **½ teaspoon black pepper**
- **½ cup all-purpose flour**
- **Olive oil**
- **1 can (14½ ounces) diced tomatoes, drained**
- **⅓ cup dry red wine**
- **⅓ cup pitted quartered Kalamata olives**
- **1 clove garlic, minced**
- **1 teaspoon chopped fresh rosemary**
- **½ teaspoon crushed red pepper flakes**
- **Cooked linguini or spaghetti**
- **Grated or shredded Parmesan cheese (optional)**

1. Season chicken with salt and pepper. Spread flour on plate, and lightly dredge chicken in flour, coating both sides.

2. Heat oil in skillet over medium heat until hot. Sear chicken in 2 or 3 batches until well browned on both sides. Use additional oil as needed to prevent sticking. Transfer to **CROCK-POT®** slow cooker.

3. Add tomatoes, wine, olives and garlic. Cover; cook on LOW 4 to 5 hours.

4. Add rosemary and red pepper flakes; stir in. Cover; cook on LOW 1 hour longer. Serve over linguini. Garnish with cheese, if desired.

Makes 4 servings

Chicken and Spicy Black Bean Tacos

1 can (15 ounces) black beans, drained and rinsed

1 can (10 ounces) tomatoes with mild green chiles, drained

1½ teaspoons chili powder

¾ teaspoon ground cumin

1 tablespoon plus 1 teaspoon extra-virgin olive oil, divided

12 ounces boneless, skinless chicken breasts, rinsed and patted dry

12 crisp corn taco shells

Optional toppings: shredded lettuce, diced tomatoes, shredded cheese, sour cream, ripe olives

1. Coat **CROCK-POT®** slow cooker with nonstick cooking spray. Add beans and tomatoes with chiles. Blend chili powder and cumin with 1 teaspoon oil and rub onto chicken breasts. Place chicken in **CROCK-POT®** slow cooker. Cover; cook on HIGH 1¾ hours.

2. Remove chicken and slice. Transfer bean mixture to bowl using slotted spoon. Stir in 1 tablespoon oil.

3. To serve, warm taco shells according to package directions. Fill with equal amounts of bean mixture and chicken. Add toppings as desired.

Makes 4 servings

Curry Chicken with Mango and Red Pepper

6 boneless, skinless chicken thighs or breasts

Salt and black pepper, to taste

Olive oil

1 bag (8 ounces) frozen mango chunks, thawed and drained

2 red bell peppers, cored, seeded and diced

1/3 cup raisins

1 shallot, thinly sliced

3/4 cup chicken broth

1 tablespoon cider vinegar

2 cloves garlic, crushed

4 thin slices fresh ginger

1 teaspoon ground cumin

1/2 teaspoon curry powder

1/2 teaspoon whole cloves

1/4 teaspoon ground red pepper (optional)

Fresh cilantro (optional)

1. Rinse, dry and season chicken with salt and pepper.

2. Heat oil in skillet over medium heat until hot. Add chicken and lightly brown, about 3 minutes per side. Transfer to **CROCK-POT**® slow cooker.

3. Add mango, bell peppers, raisins, and shallot. Combine remaining ingredients in small bowl, and pour over chicken. Cover; cook on LOW 6 to 8 hours or on HIGH 3 to 4 hours.

4. To serve, spoon mangos, raisins and cooking liquid onto chicken. Garnish with cilantro, if desired.

Makes 4 servings

Creamy Chicken and Mushrooms

1 teaspoon salt

½ teaspoon black pepper

¼ teaspoon paprika

3 boneless, skinless chicken breasts, cut into 1-inch pieces

1½ cups sliced fresh mushrooms

½ cup sliced green onions

1¾ teaspoons chicken bouillon granules

1 cup dry white wine

½ cup water

1 can (5 ounces) evaporated milk

5 teaspoons cornstarch

Hot cooked rice

1. Combine salt, pepper and paprika in small bowl; sprinkle over chicken.

2. Layer chicken, mushrooms, green onions and bouillon granules in **CROCK-POT®** slow cooker. Pour wine and water over top. Cover; cook on LOW 5 to 6 hours or on HIGH 3 hours. Remove chicken and vegetables; cover to keep warm.

3. Combine evaporated milk and cornstarch in small saucepan, stirring until smooth. Add 2 cups liquid from **CROCK-POT®** slow cooker; bring to a boil. Boil 1 minute or until thickened, stirring constantly. Serve chicken over rice and top with sauce.

Makes 3 to 4 servings

Tender Asian-Style Chicken

6 **to 8 boneless, skinless chicken thighs**

¼ **cup all-purpose flour**

½ **teaspoon black pepper**

1 **tablespoon vegetable oil**

¼ **cup soy sauce**

2 **tablespoons rice wine vinegar**

2 **tablespoons ketchup**

1 **tablespoon brown sugar**

1 **clove garlic, minced**

½ **teaspoon grated fresh ginger** *or* ¼ **teaspoon ground ginger**

¼ **teaspoon red pepper flakes**

Hot cooked rice

Chopped fresh cilantro (optional)

1. Trim fat from chicken. Combine flour and black pepper in resealable food storage bag. Add chicken; shake to coat with flour mixture.

2. Heat oil in large skillet over medium-high heat. Brown chicken about 2 minutes on each side. Place chicken in **CROCK-POT®** slow cooker. Combine soy sauce, vinegar, ketchup, sugar, garlic, ginger and pepper flakes in small bowl; pour over chicken. Cook on LOW 5 to 6 hours. Serve with rice and garnish with cilantro, if desired.

Makes 4 to 6 servings

Chicken Cacciatore

¼ **cup vegetable oil**

2½ **to 3 pounds chicken tenders, cut into bite-size pieces**

1 **can (28 ounces) crushed Italian-style tomatoes**

2 **cans (8 ounces each) Italian-style tomato sauce**

1 **medium onion, chopped**

1 **can (4 ounces) sliced mushrooms, drained**

2 **cloves garlic, minced**

1 **teaspoon salt**

1 **teaspoon dried oregano leaves**

½ **teaspoon dried thyme leaves**

½ **teaspoon black pepper**

Hot cooked spaghetti or rice

1. Heat oil in large skillet over medium-low heat. Brown chicken on all sides. Drain excess fat.

2. Transfer chicken to **CROCK-POT®** slow cooker. Add remaining ingredients except spaghetti. Cover; cook on LOW 6 to 8 hours. Serve over spaghetti.

Makes 6 to 8 servings

Chicken and Mushroom Fettuccine Alfredo

1½ **pounds chicken breast cutlets, rinsed, patted dry and cut into strips**

2 **packages (8 ounces each) cremini mushrooms, cut into thirds**

½ **teaspoon salt**

½ **teaspoon black pepper**

¼ **teaspoon garlic powder**

2 **packages (8 ounces each) cream cheese, cut into pieces**

2 **sticks butter, cut into pieces**

1½ **cups grated Parmesan cheese, plus additional for serving**

1½ **cups whole milk**

1 **box (8 ounces) fettucine noodles**

1. Spray **CROCK-POT®** slow cooker with nonstick cooking spray. Add chicken strips in single layer. Distribute mushrooms evenly over chicken. Sprinkle salt, pepper, and garlic powder over mushrooms.

2. In medium saucepan over medium heat, stir together cream cheese, butter, cheese and milk. Whisk continuously until smooth and heated through. Pour mixture over mushrooms, pushing down any mushrooms that float to top. Cover and cook on LOW 4 to 5 hours.

3. Cook fettuccine according to package directions. Drain. Add fettuccine to **CROCK-POT®** slow cooker and toss gently with sauce. Serve with Parmesan cheese.

Makes 6 to 8 servings

Traditional Cassoulet

1 **small onion, finely chopped**

2 **cloves garlic, finely chopped**

½ **cup finely chopped, peeled carrots**

½ **cup roughly chopped, seeded tomatoes**

1 **can (about 15 ounces) cannellini beans, drained and rinsed**

¼ **cup bread crumbs**

2 **tablespoons finely chopped, fresh majoram leaves**

2 **tablespoons finely chopped, fresh parsley leaves**

2 **tablespoons olive oil**

1½ **pounds chicken thighs**

½ **pound bulk pork sausage**

½ **cup dry white wine**

½ **cup chicken broth**

1. Combine onion, garlic, carrots, tomatoes, beans, bread crumbs and fresh herbs in **CROCK-POT®** slow cooker.

2. Heat olive oil in large skillet over medium-high heat. Add chicken in single layer (in batches, if necessary) and cook 3 to 4 minutes per side or until brown. Place chicken on top of mixture in **CROCK-POT®** slow cooker. Add sausage to skillet. Cook, stirring to break up meat, until cooked through. Transfer sausage to **CROCK-POT®** slow cooker with slotted spoon.

3. Return skillet to medium-high heat. Add wine and chicken broth to skillet and stir to scrape up any browned bits. Bring to a boil and cook until liquid is reduced to about one third its original volume. Remove from heat.

4. Pour reduced liquid over contents of **CROCK-POT®** slow cooker. Cover and cook on LOW 6 to 7 hours or on HIGH 3½ hours.

Makes 4 servings

Soups & Stews

TABLE OF CONTENTS

FAMILY FAVORITES..192
Classic recipes that will please the entire family

FLAVORS OF THE WORLD............................214
Best-loved cuisines from around the world

DINNER IN A BOWL 234
Rich, filling recipes sure to satisfy

HEARTY BEEF RECIPES................................ 252
Soups and stews with big, bold, beefy flavor

CHICKEN SOUPS.. 270
Simple, savory chicken soups

Family Favorites

Curried Sweet Potato and Carrot Soup

- 2 **medium-to-large sweet potatoes, peeled and cut into ¾-inch dice (about 5 cups)**
- 2 **cups baby carrots**
- 1 **small onion, chopped**
- ¾ **teaspoon curry powder**
- ½ **teaspoon salt, or to taste**
- ½ **teaspoon black pepper**
- ½ **teaspoon ground cinnamon**
- ¼ **teaspoon ground ginger**
- 4 **cups chicken broth**
- 1 **tablespoon maple syrup**
- ¾ **cup half-and-half**
  Candied ginger (optional)

1. Place sweet potatoes, carrots, onion, curry powder, salt, pepper, cinnamon and ginger in **CROCK-POT®** slow cooker. Add chicken broth. Stir well to combine. Cover; cook on LOW 7 to 8 hours.

2. Pureé soup, 1 cup at a time, in blender, returning soup to **CROCK-POT®** slow cooker after each batch. (Or, use immersion blender.) Add maple syrup and half-and-half. Add salt and pepper, if desired. Cover; cook on HIGH 15 minutes to reheat. Serve in bowls and garnish with strips or pieces of candied ginger.

Makes 8 servings

Double Corn Chowder

   2 **small celery stalks, trimmed and chopped**
   6 **ounces Canadian bacon, chopped**
   1 **small onion or 1 large shallot, chopped**
   1 **serrano chile or jalapeño pepper, cored, seeded and minced***
   1 **cup frozen corn, thawed**
   1 **cup canned hominy**
 ¼ **teaspoon salt, or to taste**
 ¼ **teaspoon crushed dried thyme**
 ¼ **teaspoon black pepper, or to taste**
   1 **cup chicken broth**
   1 **tablespoon all-purpose flour**
1½ **cups milk, divided****

*Hot peppers can sting and irritate the skin, so wear rubber gloves when handling peppers and do not touch your eyes.

**For richer chowder, use ¾ cup milk and ¾ cup half-and-half.

1. Combine celery, Canadian bacon, onion, chile pepper, corn, hominy, salt, thyme and pepper in **CROCK-POT®** slow cooker. Add broth. Cover; cook on LOW 5 to 6 hours or on HIGH 3 to 3½ hours.

2. Turn **CROCK-POT®** slow cooker to LOW. Stir together flour and 2 tablespoons milk in small bowl. Stir into corn mixture. Add remaining milk. Cover; cook on LOW 20 minutes.

Makes 4 servings

Penne Pasta Zuppa

1 **can (15 ounces) white beans, drained and rinsed**

2 **medium yellow squash, diced**

2 **ripe tomatoes, diced**

2 **small red potatoes, cubed**

2 **leeks, sliced into quarters lengthwise then chopped**

1 **carrot, peeled and diced**

¼ **pound fresh green beans, washed, stemmed and diced**

2 **fresh sage leaves, minced**

1 **teaspoon salt**

½ **teaspoon black pepper**

8 **cups water**

¼ **pound uncooked penne pasta**

Grated Romano cheese (optional)

1. Combine beans, squash, tomatoes, potatoes, leeks, carrot, green beans, sage, salt and pepper in **CROCK-POT®** slow cooker. Add water. Stir well to combine. Cover; cook on HIGH 2 hours, stirring occasionally. Turn **CROCK-POT®** slow cooker to LOW. Cook, covered, 8 hours longer. Stir occasionally.

2. Turn **CROCK-POT®** slow cooker to HIGH. Add pasta. Cover; cook 30 minutes longer or until pasta is done.

3. To serve, garnish with Romano cheese, if desired.

Makes 6 servings

Classic French Onion Soup

¼ **cup (½ stick) butter**

3 **large yellow onions, sliced**

1 **cup dry white wine**

3 **cans (about 14 ounces each) beef or chicken broth**

1 **teaspoon Worcestershire sauce**

½ **teaspoon salt**

½ **teaspoon dried thyme leaves**

4 **slices French bread, toasted**

1 **cup (4 ounces) shredded Swiss cheese**

Fresh thyme (optional)

1. Melt butter in large skillet over medium heat. Add onions, cook and stir 15 minutes or until onions are soft and lightly browned. Stir in wine.

2. Combine onion mixture, broth, Worcestershire sauce, salt and dried thyme in **CROCK-POT®** slow cooker. Cover; cook on LOW 4 to 4½ hours.

3. Ladle soup into 4 bowls; top each with bread slice and cheese. Garnish with fresh thyme, if desired.

Makes 4 servings

Butternut Squash-Apple Soup

3 **packages (12 ounces each) frozen cooked winter squash, thawed and drained** *or* **about 4½ cups mashed cooked butternut squash**

2 **cans (about 14 ounces each) chicken broth**

1 **medium Golden Delicious apple, peeled, cored and chopped**

2 **tablespoons minced onion**

1 **tablespoon packed brown sugar**

1 **teaspoon minced fresh sage** *or* **½ teaspoon ground sage**

¼ **teaspoon ground ginger**

½ **cup whipping cream or half-and-half**

1. Combine squash, broth, apple, onion, brown sugar, sage and ginger in **CROCK-POT®** slow cooker.

2. Cover; cook on LOW 6 hours or on HIGH 3 hours or until squash is tender.

3. Purée soup in food processor or blender. Stir in cream just before serving.

Makes 6 to 8 servings

Tip: For thicker soup, use only 3 cups chicken broth.

Manhattan Clam Chowder

3 slices bacon, diced

2 stalks celery, chopped

3 onions, chopped

2 cups water

1 can (15 ounces) stewed tomatoes, undrained and chopped

4 small red potatoes, diced

2 carrots, diced

½ teaspoon dried thyme

½ teaspoon black pepper

½ teaspoon Louisiana-style hot sauce

1 pound minced clams*

If fresh clams are unavailable, use canned clams; 6 (6½-ounce) cans yield about 1 pound of clam meat; drain and discard liquid.

1. Cook and stir bacon in medium saucepan until crisp. Remove bacon and place in **CROCK-POT®** slow cooker.

2. Add celery and onions to skillet. Cook and stir until tender. Place in **CROCK-POT®** slow cooker.

3. Mix in water, tomatoes with juice, potatoes, carrots, thyme, pepper and hot sauce. Cover; cook on LOW 6 to 8 hours or HIGH 4 to 6 hours. Add clams during last half hour of cooking.

Makes 4 servings

Tip: Shellfish and bivalves are delicate and should be added to the **CROCK-POT®** slow cooker during the last 15 to 30 minutes of the cooking time if you're using the HIGH heat setting, and during the last 30 to 45 minutes if you're using the LOW setting. This type of seafood overcooks easily, becoming tough and rubbery, so watch your cooking times, and cook only long enough for foods to be done.

Potato Cheddar Soup

   2 pounds red-skin potatoes, peeled and cut into ½-inch cubes

   ¾ cup coarsely chopped carrots

   1 medium onion, coarsely chopped

   3 cups chicken broth

   ½ teaspoon salt

   1 cup half-and-half

   ¼ teaspoon black pepper

   2 cups (8 ounces) shredded Cheddar cheese

1. Place potatoes, carrots, onion, broth and salt in **CROCK-POT®** slow cooker. Cover; cook on LOW 6 to 7 hours or on HIGH 3 to 3½ hours or until vegetables are tender.

2. Stir in half-and-half and pepper. Cover; cook on HIGH 15 minutes. Turn off heat and remove cover; let stand 5 minutes. Stir in cheese until melted.

Makes 6 servings

Serving suggestion: Try this soup topped with whole wheat croutons.

Vegetable Medley Soup

3 cans (about 14 ounces each) chicken broth

3 sweet potatoes, peeled and chopped

3 zucchini, chopped

2 cups chopped broccoli

2 white potatoes, peeled and shredded

1 onion, chopped

1 stalk celery, finely chopped

1 teaspoon black pepper

¼ cup (½ stick) butter, melted

2 cups half-and-half or milk

1 tablespoon salt

1 teaspoon ground cumin

1. Combine chicken broth, sweet potatoes, zucchini, broccoli, white potatoes, onion, celery, butter and pepper in **CROCK-POT®** slow cooker. Cover; cook on LOW 8 to 10 hours or on HIGH 4 to 5 hours.

2. Add half-and-half, salt and cumin. Cover; cook 30 minutes to 1 hour or until heated through.

Makes 12 servings

Granny's Apple Cidered Onion Soup with Gouda Cinnamon Toast

2 **tablespoons olive oil**

4 **tablespoons butter, cubed, divided**

4 **medium to large onions, peeled and thinly sliced**

2 **medium Granny Smith apples, peeled, cored and chopped**

4 **cups chicken broth**

1½ **cups apple cider**

2 **tablespoons brandy (optional)**

  Salt and freshly ground black pepper, to taste

6 **slices French or Italian bread, cut about ½ inch thick**

2 **tablespoons sugar**

½ **teaspoon ground cinnamon**

2 **cups shredded Gouda cheese, preferably aged**

1. Spoon oil over bottom of **CROCK-POT®** slow cooker; add 2 tablespoons butter, distributing evenly. Add onions and apples. Cover; cook on LOW 8 to 10 hours or until onions are softened and caramelized.

2. Add broth, cider and brandy, if desired. Season with salt and black pepper. Cover; cook on HIGH about 1 hour or until hot.

3. While soup is heating, make Gouda Cinnamon Toast: Preheat broiler. Spread remaining 2 tablespoons softened butter on one side of bread slices. Combine sugar and cinnamon. Sprinkle evenly over buttered bread. Place bread on baking sheet and toast under broiler until golden brown.

4. Remove from oven; turn bread over and sprinkle untoasted side with Gouda cheese. Return to broiler until cheese melts, taking care not to burn.

5. To serve, ladle soup into bowls and float 1 piece Gouda Cinnamon Toast on top of each serving, cheese side up. Serve immediately.

Makes 6 servings

Celery-Leek Bisque

3 bunches leeks (about 3 pounds), trimmed*

2 medium stalks celery, sliced

1 medium carrot, peeled and sliced

3 cloves garlic, minced

2 cans (about 14 ounces each) fat-free chicken broth

1 package (8 ounces) cream cheese with garlic and herbs

2 cups half-and-half, plus more for garnish

Salt and black pepper

Fresh basil leaves (optional)

*It is very important to rinse leeks thoroughly before using. The gritty sand in which leeks are grown can become trapped between the layers of leaves and can be difficult to see. Cut trimmed leeks in half lengthwise and submerge in several inches of cool water several times to rinse off any trapped sand.

1. Combine leeks, celery, carrots, garlic and broth in **CROCK-POT®** slow cooker. Cover and cook on LOW 8 hours or on HIGH 4 hours.

2. Purée until smooth in blender, 1 cup at a time, returning batches to **CROCK-POT®** slow cooker as they are processed. Add cream cheese to last batch in blender and purée until smooth; stir cream cheese mixture and 2 cups half-and-half into soup. Add salt and pepper to taste. Serve immediately, or cool to room temperature and refrigerate in airtight container (flavors intensify overnight). Reheat before serving. Garnish with additional half-and-half and basil leaves, if desired.

Makes 4 to 6 servings

Cauliflower Soup

2 **heads cauliflower, cut into small florets**
8 **cups chicken broth**
¾ **cup chopped celery**
¾ **cup chopped onion**
2 **teaspoons salt**
2 **teaspoons black pepper**
2 **cups milk or light cream**
1 **teaspoon Worcestershire sauce**

1. Combine cauliflower, broth, celery, onion, salt and pepper in **CROCK-POT®** slow cooker. Cover; cook on LOW 7 to 8 hours or on HIGH 3 to 4 hours.

2. Using a hand mixer or hand blender, purée soup until smooth. Mix in milk and Worcestershire sauce, continuing to blend until smooth. Cook on HIGH 15 to 20 minutes longer before serving.

Makes 8 servings

Flavors of the World

Niku Jaga (Japanese Beef Stew)

- 2 **tablespoons vegetable oil**
- 2 **pounds beef stew meat, cut in 1-inch cubes**
- 4 **medium carrots, peeled and sliced diagonally**
- 3 **medium Yukon Gold potatoes, peeled and chopped**
- 1 **white onion, peeled and chopped**
- 1 **cup water**
- ½ **cup Japanese sake** *or* ½ **cup dry white wine**
- ¼ **cup sugar**
- ¼ **cup soy sauce**
- 1 **teaspoon salt**

1. Heat oil in skillet over medium heat until hot. Sear beef on all sides, turning as it browns. Transfer beef to **CROCK-POT®** slow cooker. Add remaining ingredients. Stir well to combine.

2. Cover; cook on LOW 10 to 12 hours or on HIGH 4 to 6 hours.

Makes 6 to 8 servings

Mediterranean Shrimp Soup

2 cans (14½ ounces each) fat-free reduced-sodium chicken broth
1 can (14½ ounces) diced tomatoes
1 can (8 ounces) tomato sauce
1 medium onion, chopped
½ medium green bell pepper, chopped
½ cup orange juice
½ cup dry white wine (optional)
1 jar (2½ ounces) sliced mushrooms
¼ cup sliced pitted black olives
2 cloves garlic, minced
1 teaspoon dried basil
2 bay leaves
¼ teaspoon whole fennel seeds, crushed
⅛ teaspoon black pepper
1 pound medium raw shrimp, peeled and deveined

1. Place all ingredients except shrimp in **CROCK-POT®** slow cooker. Cover; cook on LOW 4 to 4½ hours or until vegetables are crisp-tender.

2. Stir in shrimp. Cover; cook 15 to 30 minutes or until shrimp are pink and opaque. Remove and discard bay leaves.

Makes 6 servings

Note: For a heartier soup, add 1 pound of firm white fish (such as cod or haddock), cut into 1-inch pieces, 45 minutes before end of cooking time.

Minestrone alla Milanese

1 **cup diced red potatoes**

1 **cup coarsely chopped carrots**

1 **cup coarsely chopped green cabbage**

1 **cup sliced zucchini**

¾ **cup chopped onion**

¾ **cup sliced fresh green beans**

¾ **cup coarsely chopped celery**

¾ **cup water**

2 **tablespoons olive oil**

1 **clove garlic, minced**

½ **teaspoon dried basil**

¼ **teaspoon dried rosemary**

1 **bay leaf**

2 **cans (about 14 ounces each) beef broth**

1 **can (about 14 ounces) diced tomatoes, undrained**

1 **can (15 ounces) cannellini beans, drained and rinsed**

Shredded Parmesan cheese (optional)

1. Combine all ingredients except cannellini beans and cheese in **CROCK-POT®** slow cooker; mix well. Cover; cook on LOW 5 to 6 hours.

2. Add cannellini beans. Cover; cook on LOW 1 hour or until vegetables are tender.

3. Remove and discard bay leaf. Garnish with cheese, if desired.

Makes 8 to 10 servings

French Lentil Rice Soup

6 cups chicken broth or vegetable broth

1 cup lentils, picked over and rinsed

2 medium carrots, peeled and finely diced

1 small onion, finely chopped

2 stalks celery, finely diced

3 tablespoons uncooked white rice

2 tablespoons minced garlic

1 teaspoon herbes de Provence *or* **1 teaspoon dried thyme**

½ teaspoon salt

⅛ teaspoon ground white pepper*

¼ cup heavy cream *or* **¼ cup sour cream, divided (optional)**

¼ cup chopped parsley (optional)

*Substitute black pepper, if desired.

1. Stir together broth, lentils, carrots, onion, celery, rice, garlic, herbes de Provence, salt and pepper in **CROCK-POT®** slow cooker. Cover and cook on LOW 8 hours or on HIGH 4 to 5 hours.

2. Remove 1½ cups soup and purée in food processor or blender until almost smooth.** Stir puréed soup back into **CROCK-POT®** slow cooker.

3. Divide soup evenly among four serving bowls garnishing each with 1 tablespoon cream and 1 tablespoon chopped parsley, if desired.

Makes 4 servings

**Use caution when processing hot liquids in blender. Vent lid of blender and cover with clean kitchen towel as directed by manufacturer.

Black Bean Chipotle Soup

1 **pound dry black beans**

2 **stalks celery, cut into ¼-inch dice**

2 **carrots, cut into ¼-inch dice**

1 **yellow onion, cut into ¼-inch dice**

2 **chipotle peppers in adobo sauce, chopped**

1 **cup crushed tomatoes**

1 **can (4 ounces) diced mild green chiles, drained**

6 **cups chicken or vegetable stock**

2 **teaspoons cumin**

Salt and black pepper, to taste

Optional toppings: sour cream, chunky-style salsa, fresh chopped cilantro

1. Rinse and sort beans and place in large bowl; cover completely with water. Soak 6 to 8 hours or overnight. (To quick-soak beans, place beans in large saucepan; cover with water. Bring to a boil over high heat. Boil 2 minutes. Remove from heat; let soak, covered, 1 hour.) Drain beans; discard water.

2. Place beans in **CROCK-POT®** slow cooker. Add celery, carrots and onion.

3. Combine chipotles, tomatoes, chiles, stock and cumin in medium bowl. Add to **CROCK-POT®** slow cooker. Cover; cook on LOW 7 to 8 hours or on HIGH 4½ to 5 hours, or until beans are tender. Season with salt and pepper.

4. If desired, process mixture in blender, in 2 or 3 batches, to desired consistency, or leave chunky. Serve with sour cream, salsa and cilantro, if desired.

Makes 4 to 6 servings

Tip: For an even heartier soup stir in 1 cup diced, browned spicy sausage, such as linguiça or chorizo, before serving.

Russian Borscht

   4 cups thinly sliced green cabbage
1½ pounds fresh beets, shredded
   5 small carrots, halved lengthwise then cut into 1-inch pieces
   1 parsnip, peeled, halved lengthwise then cut into 1-inch pieces
   1 cup chopped onion
   4 cloves garlic, minced
   1 pound beef stew meat, cut into ½-inch cubes
   1 can (about 14 ounces) diced tomatoes
   3 cans (about 14 ounces each) reduced-sodium beef broth
 ¼ cup lemon juice, or more to taste
   1 tablespoon sugar, or more to taste
   1 teaspoon black pepper
      Sour cream (optional)
      Fresh parsley (optional)

1. Layer ingredients in **CROCK-POT®** slow cooker in following order: cabbage, beets, carrots, parsnip, onion, garlic, beef, tomatoes, broth, lemon juice, sugar and pepper. Cover; cook on LOW 7 to 9 hours or until vegetables are crisp-tender.

2. Season with additional lemon juice and sugar, if desired. Dollop each serving with sour cream and sprinkle with parsley, if desired.

Makes 12 servings

Tuscany Bean and Prosciutto Soup

- **2 tablespoons unsalted butter**
- **4 slices prosciutto***
- **3 cups water**
- **1 cup dried navy beans, rinsed and sorted**
- **½ cup dried lima beans, rinsed and sorted**
- **1 medium yellow onion, finely chopped**
- **1 tablespoon chopped fresh cilantro**
- **1 teaspoon salt**
- **1 teaspoon ground cumin**
- **1 teaspoon black pepper**
- **½ teaspoon ground paprika**
- **2 cans (15 ounces each) diced tomatoes, undrained**

Substitute 4 slices bacon, if desired

1. Melt butter in large skillet over medium-high heat. Add prosciutto and fry until crisp. Remove to paper towels to cool.

2. Crumble prosciutto into small pieces in **CROCK-POT®** slow cooker. Add water, navy beans, lima beans, onion, cilantro, salt, cumin, black pepper and paprika. Stir well to combine. Cover and cook on LOW 10 to 12 hours.

3. Add tomatoes and juice and stir well. Cover and cook on HIGH 30 to 40 minutes or until soup is heated through.

Makes 6 servings

Greek Lemon and Rice Soup

3 cans (about 14 ounces each) chicken broth

½ cup long-grain white rice (not converted or instant rice)

3 egg yolks

¼ cup fresh lemon juice

¼ teaspoon salt

⅛ teaspoon ground white pepper*

4 thin slices lemon (optional)

4 teaspoons finely chopped parsley (optional)

Substitute black pepper if desired.

1. Stir chicken broth and rice together in **CROCK-POT**® slow cooker. Cover and cook on HIGH 2 to 3 hours or until rice is cooked.

2. Turn to LOW. Whisk egg yolks and lemon juice together in medium bowl. Whisk large spoonful of hot rice mixture into egg yolk mixture. Whisk back into **CROCK-POT**® slow cooker.

3. Cook on LOW 10 minutes. Season with salt and pepper. Ladle soup into serving bowls and garnish each bowl with thin slice of lemon and 1 teaspoon chopped parsley, if desired.

Makes 4 servings

Note: Soup may be served hot or cold. To serve cold, allow soup to cool to room temperature. Cover and refrigerate up to 24 hours before serving.

Italian Hillside Garden Soup

1 tablespoon extra-virgin olive oil

1 cup chopped green bell pepper

1 cup chopped onion

½ cup sliced celery

1 can (about 14 ounces) diced tomatoes with basil, garlic and oregano, undrained

1 can (15½ ounces) navy beans, drained and rinsed

1 medium zucchini, chopped

1 cup frozen cut green beans, thawed

2 cans (about 14 ounces each) chicken broth

¼ teaspoon garlic powder

1 package (9 ounces) refrigerated sausage- and cheese-filled tortellini pasta

3 tablespoons chopped fresh basil

Grated Asiago or Parmesan cheese (optional)

1. Heat oil in large skillet over medium-high heat. Add bell pepper, onion and celery; cook and stir 4 minutes or until onions are translucent. Remove mixture to **CROCK-POT**® slow cooker.

2. Add tomatoes with juice, navy beans, zucchini, green beans, broth and garlic powder. Cover; cook on LOW 7 hours or on HIGH 3½ hours.

3. Turn **CROCK-POT**® slow cooker to HIGH. Stir in tortellini. Cover; cook on HIGH 20 to 25 minutes or until pasta is tender. Stir in basil. Garnish each serving with cheese.

Makes 6 servings

Tip: Cooking times are guidelines. **CROCK-POT**® slow cookers, just like ovens, cook differently depending on a variety of factors, including capacity. For example, cooking times will be longer at high altitudes.

Fresh Lime and Black Bean Soup

2 cans (15 ounces each) black beans, undrained

1 can (14½ ounces) reduced-sodium chicken broth

1½ cups chopped onion

1½ teaspoons chili powder

¾ teaspoon ground cumin

¼ teaspoon garlic powder

⅛ to ¼ teaspoon red pepper flakes

½ cup sour cream

2 tablespoons extra-virgin olive oil

2 tablespoons chopped cilantro

1 medium lime, cut into wedges

1. Coat **CROCK-POT®** slow cooker with nonstick cooking spray. Add beans, broth, onion, chili powder, cumin, garlic powder and pepper flakes. Cover; cook on LOW 7 hours or on HIGH 3½ hours, or until onions are very soft.

2. Process 1 cup soup mixture in blender until smooth and return to **CROCK-POT®** slow cooker. Stir, check consistency, and repeat with additional 1 cup soup, as needed to achieve desired consistency. Let stand 15 to 20 minutes before serving.

3. Ladle soup into 4 bowls. Divide sour cream, oil and cilantro evenly among servings. Squeeze juice from lime wedge over each.

Makes 4 servings

Tip: Brighten the flavor of dishes cooked in the **CROCK-POT®** slow cooker by adding fresh herbs or fresh lemon or lime juice just before serving.

Dinner in a Bowl

Hearty Mushroom and Barley Soup

- 9 **cups chicken broth**
- 1 **package (16 ounces) sliced fresh button mushrooms**
- 1 **large onion, chopped**
- 2 **carrots, chopped**
- 2 **stalks celery, chopped**
- ½ **cup uncooked pearl barley**
- ½ **ounce dried porcini mushrooms**
- 3 **cloves garlic, minced**
- 1 **teaspoon salt**
- ½ **teaspoon dried thyme**
- ½ **teaspoon black pepper**

Combine all ingredients in **CROCK-POT®** slow cooker; stir until well blended. Cover; cook on LOW 4 to 6 hours.

Makes 8 to 10 servings

Variation: For even more flavor, add a beef or ham bone to the **CROCK-POT®** slow cooker with the rest of the ingredients.

Hearty Lentil and Root Vegetable Stew

2 cans (about 14 ounces each) chicken broth

1½ cups diced turnip

1 cup dried red lentils, rinsed and sorted

1 medium onion, cut into ½-inch wedges

2 medium carrots, cut into 1-inch pieces

1 medium red bell pepper, cut into 1-inch pieces

½ teaspoon dried oregano

⅛ teaspoon red pepper flakes

1 tablespoon olive oil

½ teaspoon salt

4 slices bacon, crisp-cooked and crumbled

½ cup finely chopped green onions

1. Combine broth, turnips, lentils, onion, carrots, bell pepper, oregano and pepper flakes in **CROCK-POT®** slow cooker. Cover; cook on LOW 6 hours or on HIGH 3 hours or until lentils are cooked.

2. Stir in olive oil and salt. Sprinkle each serving with bacon and green onions.

Makes 8 servings

Linguiça & Green Bean Soup

1 **large yellow onion, chopped**

3 **cloves garlic, minced**

2 **tablespoons olive oil**

1 **cup tomato juice**

4 **cups water**

1 **tablespoon Italian seasoning**

2 **teaspoons garlic salt**

1 **teaspoon ground cumin**

1 **bay leaf**

2 **cans (16 ounces each) cut green beans, drained**

1 **can (16 ounces) kidney beans, drained**

1 **pound linguiça sausage, cooked and cut into bite-sized pieces**

Place all ingredients in **CROCK-POT®** slow cooker. Cover; cook on LOW 8 to 10 hours or on HIGH 4 to 6 hours. Add more boiling water during cooking, if necessary.

Makes 6 servings

Tip: Serve with warm cornbread.

Hearty Meatball Stew

  3 **pounds ground beef or ground turkey**
  1 **cup Italian bread crumbs**
  4 **eggs**
  ½ **cup milk**
  ¼ **cup grated Romano cheese**
  2 **teaspoons salt**
  2 **teaspoons garlic salt**
  2 **teaspoons black pepper**
  2 **tablespoons olive oil**
  2 **cups water**
  2 **cups beef broth**
  1 **can (14½ ounces) stewed tomatoes, undrained**
  1 **can (12 ounces) tomato paste**
  1 **cup chopped carrots**
  1 **cup chopped onions**
  ¼ **cup chopped celery**
  1 **tablespoon Italian seasoning**

1. Combine beef, bread crumbs, eggs, milk, cheese, salt, garlic salt and pepper in large bowl. Form into 2-inch-round balls. Heat oil in skillet over medium-high heat until hot. Brown meatballs on all sides. Transfer to **CROCK-POT®** slow cooker.

2. Add remaining ingredients. Stir well to combine. Cover; cook on LOW 4 to 6 hours or on HIGH 2 to 4 hours.

Makes 6 to 8 servings

My Mother's Sausage and Vegetable Soup

1 **can (15 ounces) black beans, drained and rinsed**
1 **can (about 14 ounces) diced tomatoes**
1 **can (10¾ ounces) condensed cream of mushroom soup, undiluted**
½ **pound smoked turkey sausage, cut into ½-inch slices**
2 **cups diced potato**
1 **cup chopped onion**
1 **cup chopped red bell pepper**
½ **cup water**
2 **teaspoons extra-hot prepared horseradish**
2 **teaspoons honey**
1 **teaspoon dried basil**

Combine all ingredients in **CROCK-POT®** slow cooker, mix well. Cover; cook on LOW 7 to 8 hours or until potato is tender.

Makes 6 to 8 servings

Rich and Hearty Drumstick Soup

2 **turkey drumsticks (about 1¾ pounds total)**

2 **medium carrots, peeled and sliced**

1 **medium stalk celery, thinly sliced**

1 **cup chopped onion**

1 **teaspoon minced garlic**

½ **teaspoon poultry seasoning**

4½ **cups chicken broth**

2 **ounces uncooked dry egg noodles**

¼ **cup chopped parsley**

2 **tablespoons butter**

¾ **teaspoon salt, or to taste**

1. Coat **CROCK-POT®** slow cooker with nonstick cooking spray. Add drumsticks, carrots, celery, onion, garlic and poultry seasoning. Pour broth over; cover. Cook on HIGH 5 hours or until turkey meat is falling off bones.

2. Remove turkey; set aside. Add noodles to **CROCK-POT®** slow cooker; cover and cook 30 minutes more or until noodles are tender. Meanwhile, debone turkey and cut meat into bite-size pieces; set meat aside.

3. When noodles are cooked, stir in turkey, parsley, butter and salt.

Makes 4 servings

Navy Bean Bacon Chowder

1½ **cups dried navy beans**

2 **cups cold water**

6 **slices thick-cut bacon**

1 **medium carrot, cut lengthwise into halves, then cut into 1-inch pieces**

1 **small turnip, cut into 1-inch pieces**

1 **stalk celery, chopped**

1 **medium onion, chopped**

1 **teaspoon Italian seasoning**

⅛ **teaspoon black pepper**

1 **can (46 ounces) reduced-sodium chicken broth**

1 **cup milk**

1. Soak beans overnight in cold water; drain.

2. Cook bacon in medium skillet over medium heat. Drain fat; crumble bacon into **CROCK-POT®** slow cooker. Stir in beans, carrot, turnip, celery, onion, Italian seasoning and pepper. Add broth. Cover; cook on LOW 8 to 9 hours or until beans are tender.

3. Ladle 2 cups of soup mixture into food processor or blender. Process until smooth; return to **CROCK-POT®** slow cooker. Add milk. Cover; cook on HIGH 15 minutes or until heated through.

Makes 6 servings

Cape Cod Stew

½ **pound uncooked shrimp, peeled, cleaned and deveined**

½ **pound fresh cod or other white fish**

1 **pound mussels or hard-shell clams**

2 **cans (14½ ounces each) diced tomatoes, undrained**

4 **cups beef broth**

½ **cup chopped onions**

½ **cup chopped carrots**

½ **cup chopped cilantro**

2 **tablespoons sea salt**

2 **teaspoons crushed or minced garlic**

2 **teaspoons lemon juice**

4 **whole bay leaves**

1 **teaspoon dried thyme**

½ **teaspoon saffron**

1. Cut shrimp and fish into bite-size chunks and place in large bowl; refrigerate. Place mussels in second large bowl and set aside in refrigerator.

2. Combine remaining ingredients in **CROCK-POT®** slow cooker. Cover; cook on LOW 7 hours.

3. Add seafood. Cover; cook on HIGH 15 to 30 minutes or until seafood is just cooked through.

Makes 8 servings

Beggar's Chowder

¼ cup unsalted butter, at room temperature

¼ cup all-purpose flour

1 tablespoon garlic salt

1 tablespoon thyme

1 tablespoon sweet Hungarian paprika

½ teaspoon coarsely ground black pepper

4 skinless bone-in turkey legs or thighs, trimmed of visible fat

2 cans (14½ ounces each) cream-style sweet corn

1 can (10¾ ounces) condensed chicken broth, undiluted

1½ cups diced yellow onion

1 cup diced red bell pepper

1 cup diced green bell pepper

1 pound cleaned, stemmed white mushrooms, halved or quartered if large

1 can (14½ ounces) petite diced tomatoes, drained

1½ cups heavy whipping cream

½ cup chopped cilantro or parsley, plus additional for garnish

Salt and black pepper, to taste

1. Coat **CROCK-POT**® slow cooker with nonstick cooking spray. Combine butter, flour, garlic salt, thyme, paprika and pepper in small bowl. Use back of wooden spoon to work mixture into smooth paste. Rub paste into all sides of turkey.

2. Place turkey in **CROCK-POT**® slow cooker. Add corn, broth, onion and bell peppers.

3. Cover; cook on HIGH 3 hours or until turkey is fork-tender. Remove turkey; set aside until cool enough to handle.

4. Add mushrooms and tomatoes to cooking liquid. Cover; cook on HIGH 30 minutes longer.

5. Meanwhile, remove turkey meat from bones in bite-size pieces. When mushrooms are tender, return turkey to **CROCK-POT**® slow cooker. Add cream and cilantro. Cook, covered, about 15 minutes or until heated through. Add salt and pepper, if desired. Garnish with additional chopped cilantro, if desired.

Makes 8 servings

Hearty Beef Recipes

Mexican Cheese Soup

1 **pound processed cheese, cubed**

1 **pound ground beef, cooked and drained**

1 **can (8¾ ounces) whole kernel corn, undrained**

1 **can (15 ounces) kidney beans, undrained**

1 **jalapeño pepper, seeded and diced (optional)***

1 **can (14½ ounces) diced tomatoes with green chiles, undrained**

1 **can (14½ ounces) stewed tomatoes, undrained**

1 **envelope taco seasoning**

Jalapeño peppers can sting and irritate the skin; wear rubber gloves when handling peppers and do not touch eyes. Wash hands after handling.

1. Coat inside of **CROCK-POT**® slow cooker with nonstick cooking spray. Combine cheese, beef, corn, beans with liquid, jalapeño, if desired, tomatoes with chiles, stewed tomatoes and taco seasoning in prepared **CROCK-POT**® slow cooker.

2. Cover; cook on LOW 4 to 5 hours or on HIGH 3 hours or until done.

Makes 6 to 8 servings

Serving Suggestion: Corn chips make an excellent accompaniment to this hearty soup.

Asian Beef Stew

2 onions, cut into ¼-inch slices

1½ pounds round steak, sliced thin across the grain

2 stalks celery, sliced

2 carrots, peeled and sliced *or* 1 cup peeled baby carrots

1 cup sliced mushrooms

1 cup orange juice

1 cup beef broth

⅓ cup hoisin sauce*

2 tablespoons cornstarch

1 to 2 teaspoons Chinese five-spice powder* *or* curry powder

1 cup frozen peas

Hot cooked rice

Chopped fresh cilantro (optional)

Available in the Asian foods aisle of your local market.

1. Place onions, beef, celery, carrots and mushrooms in **CROCK-POT®** slow cooker.

2. Combine orange juice, broth, hoisin sauce, cornstarch and five-spice powder in small bowl. Pour into **CROCK-POT®** slow cooker. Cover; cook on HIGH 5 hours or until beef is tender.

3. Stir in peas. Cook 20 minutes longer or until peas are tender. Serve with hot cooked rice, and garnish with cilantro, if desired.

Makes 6 servings

Hamburger Soup

- 1 **pound lean ground beef**
- 1 **cup thinly sliced carrots**
- 1 **cup sliced celery**
- 1 **package (1 ounce) dry onion soup mix**
- 1 **package (1 ounce) Italian salad dressing mix**
- ¼ **teaspoon seasoned salt**
- ¼ **teaspoon black pepper**
- 3 **cups boiling water**
- 1 **can (about 14 ounces) diced tomatoes, undrained**
- 1 **can (8 ounces) tomato sauce**
- 1 **tablespoon soy sauce**
- 2 **cups cooked macaroni**
- ¼ **cup grated Parmesan cheese**
- 2 **tablespoons chopped fresh parsley**

1. Brown ground beef in large skillet 6 to 8 minutes over medium-high heat, stirring to break up meat. Drain fat.

2. Place carrots and celery in **CROCK-POT**® slow cooker. Top with beef, soup mix, salad dressing mix, seasoned salt and pepper. Add water, tomatoes with juice, tomato sauce and soy sauce; mix well. Cover; cook on LOW 6 to 8 hours.

3. Stir in macaroni and Parmesan cheese. Cover; cook on HIGH 15 to 30 minutes or until heated through. Sprinkle with parsley just before serving.

Makes 6 to 8 servings

Grandma Ruth's Minestrone

1 **pound ground beef**

1 **cup dried red kidney beans**

1 **package (16 ounces) frozen mixed vegetables**

2 **cans (8 ounces each) tomato sauce**

1 **can (about 14 ounces) diced tomatoes, undrained**

¼ **head shredded cabbage**

1 **cup chopped onions**

1 **cup chopped celery**

½ **cup chopped fresh parsley**

1 **tablespoon dried basil**

1 **tablespoon Italian seasoning**

1 **teaspoon salt**

1 **teaspoon black pepper**

1 **cup cooked macaroni**

1. Combine ground beef and beans in **CROCK-POT®** slow cooker. Cover; cook on HIGH 2 hours.

2. Add all remaining ingredients except macaroni and stir to blend. Cover; cook on LOW for 6 to 8 hours or until beans are tender.

3. Stir macaroni into slow cooker. Cover; cook on HIGH for 1 hour.

Makes 4 servings

Hamburger Veggie Soup

1 pound 95% lean ground beef

1 bag (16 ounces) frozen mixed vegetables

1 package (10 ounces) frozen seasoning-blend vegetables*

1 can (10¾ ounces) condensed tomato soup, undiluted

1 can (about 14 ounces) stewed tomatoes, undrained

2 cans (5½ ounces each) spicy vegetable juice

Salt and black pepper, to taste

*Seasoning-blend vegetables are a mixture of chopped bell peppers, onions and celery. If you're unable to find frozen vegetables, use ½ cup of each fresh vegetable.

Coat **CROCK-POT®** slow cooker with nonstick cooking spray. Crumble beef before placing in bottom. Add remaining ingredients. Stir well to blend. Cover; cook on HIGH 4 hours. If necessary, break up large pieces of beef. Add salt and pepper before serving, if desired.

Makes 4 to 6 servings

Sweet and Sour Brisket Stew

 1 **jar (12 ounces) chili sauce**
1½ **to 2 tablespoons packed dark brown sugar**
1½ **tablespoons fresh lemon juice**
 ¼ **cup beef broth**
 1 **tablespoon Dijon mustard**
 ¼ **teaspoon paprika**
 ½ **teaspoon salt, or to taste**
 ¼ **teaspoon black pepper, or to taste**
 1 **clove garlic, minced**
 1 **small onion, chopped**
 1 **well-trimmed beef brisket, cut into 1-inch pieces***
 2 **large carrots, cut into ½-inch slices**
 1 **tablespoon all-purpose flour (optional)**

Beef brisket has a heavy layer of fat, which some supermarkets trim off. If the meat is trimmed, buy 2½ pounds; if not, purchase 4 pounds, then trim and discard excess fat.

1. Combine sauce, 1½ tablespoons brown sugar, lemon juice, broth, mustard, paprika, salt and pepper in **CROCK-POT®** slow cooker. (Add remaining sugar, if desired, after tasting.)

2. Add garlic, onion, beef and carrots. Stir well to coat. Cover; cook on LOW 8 hours.

3. If thicker gravy is desired, whisk together 1 tablespoon flour and 3 tablespoons cooking liquid in small bowl. Add to **CROCK-POT®** slow cooker. Cover; cook on HIGH 10 minutes, or until thickened.

Makes 6 to 8 servings

Wild Mushroom Beef Stew

1½ **to 2 pounds beef stew meat, cut into 1-inch cubes**
2 **tablespoons all-purpose flour**
½ **teaspoon salt**
½ **teaspoon black pepper**
1½ **cups beef broth**
1 **teaspoon Worcestershire sauce**
1 **clove garlic, minced**
1 **bay leaf**
1 **teaspoon paprika**
4 **shiitake mushrooms, sliced**
2 **medium carrots, sliced**
2 **medium potatoes, diced**
1 **small white onion, chopped**
1 **stalk celery, sliced**

1. Place beef in **CROCK-POT®** slow cooker. Mix together flour, salt and pepper and sprinkle over beef; stir to coat evenly. Add remaining ingredients and stir to mix well.

2. Cover; cook on LOW 10 to 12 hours or on HIGH for 4 to 6 hours. Stir the stew before serving.

Makes 5 servings

Note: This classic beef stew is given a twist with the addition of flavorful shiitake mushrooms. If shiitake mushrooms are unavailable in your local grocery store, you can substitute other mushrooms of your choice. For extra punch, add a few dried porcini mushrooms to the stew.

Tip: You may double the amount of meat, mushrooms, carrots, potatoes, onion and celery for a 5-, 6- or 7-quart **CROCK-POT®** slow cooker.

Beef Fajita Soup

1 **pound beef stew meat**

1 **can (15 ounces) pinto beans, drained and rinsed**

1 **can (15 ounces) black beans, drained and rinsed**

1 **can (about 14 ounces) diced tomatoes with roasted garlic, undrained**

1 **can (about 14 ounces) beef broth**

1 **small green bell pepper, thinly sliced**

1 **small red bell pepper, thinly sliced**

1 **small onion, thinly sliced**

1½ **cups water**

2 **teaspoons ground cumin**

1 **teaspoon seasoned salt**

1 **teaspoon black pepper**

Combine beef, beans, tomatoes with juice, broth, bell peppers, onion, water, cumin, salt and black pepper in **CROCK-POT®** slow cooker. Cover; cook on LOW 8 hours.

Makes 8 servings

Serving Suggestion: Serve topped with sour cream, shredded Monterey Jack or Cheddar cheese and chopped olives.

Beef Stew with Molasses and Raisins

1/3 **cup all-purpose flour**

2 **teaspoons salt, divided**

1½ **teaspoons black pepper, divided**

2 **pounds beef stew meat, cut into 1½-inch pieces**

5 **tablespoons oil, divided**

2 **medium onions, sliced**

1 **can (28 ounces) diced tomatoes, drained**

1 **cup beef broth**

3 **tablespoons molasses**

2 **tablespoons cider vinegar**

4 **cloves garlic, minced**

2 **teaspoons dried thyme**

1 **teaspoon celery salt**

1 **bay leaf**

8 **ounces baby carrots, cut in half lengthwise**

2 **parsnips, diced**

½ **cup golden raisins**

1. Combine flour, 1½ teaspoons salt and 1 teaspoon pepper in large bowl. Toss meat in flour mixture. Heat 2 tablespoons oil in large skillet or Dutch oven over medium-high heat until hot. Add half of beef and brown on all sides. Set aside browned beef and repeat with 2 additional tablespoons oil and remaining beef.

2. Add remaining 1 tablespoon oil to skillet. Add onions and cook, stirring to loosen any browned bits, about 5 minutes. Add tomatoes, broth, molasses, vinegar, garlic, thyme, celery salt, bay leaf and remaining ½ teaspoon salt and ½ teaspoon pepper. Bring to a boil. Add browned beef and boil 1 minute.

3. Transfer to **CROCK-POT®** slow cooker. Cover; cook on LOW 5 hours or on HIGH 2½ hours. Add carrots, parsnips and raisins. Cook 1 to 2 hours longer or until vegetables are tender. Remove and discard bay leaf.

Makes 6 to 8 servings

Chicken Soups

Hearty Chicken Tequila Soup

- 1 **small onion, cut into 8 wedges**
- 1 **cup frozen corn, thawed**
- 1 **can (14½ ounces) diced tomatoes with mild green chiles, undrained**
- 2 **cloves garlic, minced**
- 2 **tablespoons chopped fresh cilantro, plus additional for garnish**
- 1 **whole chicken (about 3½ pounds)**
- 2 **cups chicken broth**
- 3 **tablespoons tequila**
- ¼ **cup sour cream**

1. Spread onions in bottom of **CROCK-POT®** slow cooker. Add corn, tomatoes with chiles, garlic and 2 tablespoons cilantro. Mix well to combine. Place chicken on top of tomato mixture.

2. Combine broth and tequila in medium bowl. Pour over chicken. Cover; cook on LOW 8 to 10 hours.

3. Transfer chicken to cutting board and let rest until cool enough to handle. Remove skin and bones. Pull meat apart with 2 forks into bite-size pieces. Return chicken to **CROCK-POT®** slow cooker and stir.

4. Serve with dollop of sour cream and garnish with cilantro.

Makes 2 to 4 servings

Chicken & Barley Soup

1 **cup thinly sliced celery**

1 **medium onion, coarsely chopped**

1 **carrot, cut into thin slices**

½ **cup medium pearl barley**

1 **clove garlic, minced**

1 **cut-up whole chicken (about 3 pounds)**

1 **tablespoon olive oil**

2½ **cups chicken broth**

1 **can (about 14 ounces) diced tomatoes, undrained**

¾ **teaspoon salt**

½ **teaspoon dried basil**

¼ **teaspoon black pepper**

1. Place celery, onion, carrot, barley and garlic in **CROCK-POT®** slow cooker.

2. Remove and discard skin from chicken pieces. Separate drumsticks from thighs. Trim back bone from breasts. Save wings for another use. Heat oil in large skillet over medium-high heat; brown chicken pieces on all sides. Place chicken in **CROCK-POT®** slow cooker.

3. Add broth, tomatoes with juice, salt, basil and pepper. Cook on LOW 7 to 8 hours or HIGH 4 hours or until chicken and barley are tender. Remove chicken and debone. Cut chicken into bite-size pieces; stir into soup.

Makes 4 servings

Country Chicken Chowder

2 tablespoons margarine or butter

1½ pounds boneless, skinless chicken breast tenders, cut into ½-inch pieces

2 small onions, chopped

2 stalks celery, sliced

2 small carrots, peeled and sliced

2 cups frozen corn

2 cans (10¾ ounces each) condensed cream of potato soup, undiluted

1½ cups chicken broth

1 teaspoon dried dill weed

½ cup half-and-half

1. Melt margarine in large skillet. Add chicken; cook until browned.

2. Add cooked chicken, onions, celery, carrots, corn, soup, chicken broth and dill to **CROCK-POT®** slow cooker. Cover and cook on LOW 3 to 4 hours or until chicken is no longer pink and vegetables are tender.

3. Turn off heat; stir in half-and-half. Cover and let stand 5 to 10 minutes or just until heated through.

Makes 8 servings

Note: For a special touch, garnish soup with croutons and fresh dill.

Chicken Fiesta Soup

    4 boneless, skinless chicken breasts, cooked and shredded
    1 can (14½ ounces) stewed tomatoes, drained
    2 cans (4 ounces each) chopped green chiles, drained
    1 can (28 ounces) enchilada sauce
    1 can (14½ ounces) chicken broth
    1 cup finely chopped onions
    2 cloves garlic, minced
    1 teaspoon ground cumin
    1 teaspoon chili powder
  ¾ teaspoon black pepper
    1 teaspoon salt
  ¼ cup finely chopped fresh cilantro
    1 cup frozen whole kernel corn
    1 yellow squash, diced
    1 zucchini, diced
    8 tostada shells, crumbled
    2 cups (8 ounces) shredded Cheddar cheese

1. Combine chicken, tomatoes, chiles, enchilada sauce, broth, onions, garlic, cumin, chili powder, pepper, salt, cilantro, corn, squash and zucchini, in **CROCK-POT®** slow cooker.

2. Cover; cook on LOW 8 hours. To serve, fill individual bowls with soup. Garnish with crumbled tostada shells and cheese.

Makes 8 servings

Chicken and Wild Rice Soup

3 cans (about 14 ounces each) chicken broth

1 pound boneless, skinless chicken breasts or thighs, cut into bite-size pieces

2 cups water

1 cup sliced celery

1 cup diced carrots

1 package (6 ounces) converted long grain and wild rice mix with seasoning packet (not quick-cooking or instant rice)

½ cup chopped onion

½ teaspoon black pepper

2 teaspoons white vinegar (optional)

1 tablespoon dried parsley flakes

1. Combine broth, chicken, water, celery, carrots, rice mix and seasoning packet, onion and pepper in **CROCK-POT®** slow cooker; mix well.

2. Cover; cook on LOW 6 to 7 hours or on HIGH 4 to 5 hours or until chicken is tender.

3. Stir in vinegar, if desired. Sprinkle with parsley.

Makes 9 servings

Creamy Farmhouse Chicken and Garden Soup

½ (16-ounce) package frozen pepper stir-fry vegetable mix

1 cup frozen corn

1 medium zucchini, sliced

2 bone-in chicken thighs, skinned

½ teaspoon minced garlic

1 can (about 14 ounces) fat-free chicken broth

½ teaspoon dried thyme

2 ounces uncooked egg noodles

1 cup half-and-half

½ cup frozen green peas, thawed

2 tablespoons chopped parsley

2 tablespoons butter, melted

1 teaspoon salt

½ teaspoon coarsely ground black pepper

1. Coat **CROCK-POT®** slow cooker with nonstick cooking spray. Place stir-fry vegetables, corn and zucchini in bottom. Add chicken, garlic, broth and thyme. Cover; cook on HIGH 3 to 4 hours or until chicken is no longer pink. Remove chicken and set aside to cool slightly.

2. Add noodles to **CROCK-POT®** slow cooker. Cover; cook 20 minutes longer, or until noodles are done.

3. Meanwhile, debone and chop chicken. Return to **CROCK-POT®** slow cooker. Stir in remaining ingredients. Let stand 5 minutes before serving.

Makes 4 servings

Note: To skin chicken easily, grasp skin with paper towel and pull away. Repeat with fresh paper towel for each piece of chicken, discarding skins and towels.

Index

A

Almonds: Chicken Sausage Pilaf, 50
Angel Wings, 106
Asian Barbecue Skewers, 102
Asian Beef Stew, 254
Asian Beef with Broccoli, 62
Asian Chicken "Fondue," 115
Asian Lettuce Wraps, 112
Autumn Chicken, 162

B

Bacon
Bacon and Onion Brisket, 24
Coq au Vin, 148
Hearty Lentil and Root Vegetable Stew, 236
Heidi's Chicken Supreme, 52
Manhattan Clam Chowder, 202
Navy Bean Bacon Chowder, 246
Bacon and Onion Brisket, 24
Barley
Barley with Currants and Pine Nuts, 70
Chicken & Barley Soup, 272
Hearty Mushroom and Barley Soup, 234
Barley with Currants and Pine Nuts, 70
Basque Chicken with Peppers, 152
Beans, Black
Beef Fajita Soup, 266
Black and White Chili, 118
Black Bean Chipotle Soup, 222
Chicken and Black Bean Chili, 134
Chicken and Spicy Black Bean Tacos, 180

Beans, Black *(continued)*
Chipotle Chicken Casserole, 161
Chipotle Chicken Stew, 126
Fresh Lime and Black Bean Soup, 232
My Mother's Sausage and Vegetable Soup, 242
Beans, Cannellini
Minestrone alla Milanese, 218
Quatro Frijoles con Pollo Cantaro, 128
Traditional Cassoulet, 190
Beans, Chili: Chorizo Chili, 36
Beans, Garbanzo: Quatro Frijoles con Pollo Cantaro, 128
Beans, Great Northern
Black and White Chili, 118
Pesto Rice and Beans, 78
Quatro Frijoles con Pollo Cantaro, 128
Beans, Green
Italian Hillside Garden Soup, 230
Linguiça & Green Bean Soup, 238
Minestrone alla Milanese, 218
Penne Pasta Zuppa, 196
Pesto Rice and Beans, 78
Beans, Kidney
Grandma Ruth's Minestrone, 258
Linguiça & Green Bean Soup, 238
Mexican Cheese Soup, 252
Mile-High Enchilada Pie, 69
Quatro Frijoles con Pollo Cantaro, 128

Beans, Lima: Tuscany Bean and Prosciutto Soup, 226
Beans, Navy
Chipotle Chicken Casserole, 161
Chipotle Chicken Stew, 126
Italian Hillside Garden Soup, 230
Navy Bean Bacon Chowder, 246
Tuscany Bean and Prosciutto Soup, 226
Beans, Pinto: Beef Fajita Soup, 266
Beans, White: Penne Pasta Zuppa, 196
Beef *(see also **Beef, Ground**)*
Asian Beef Stew, 254
Asian Beef with Broccoli, 62
Bacon and Onion Brisket, 24
Beef Fajita Soup, 266
Beef Stew with Molasses and Raisins, 268
Best-Ever Roast, 8
Carne Rellenos, 58
Corned Beef and Cabbage, 56
Country-Style Steak, 16
Dad's Dill Beef Roast, 12
Easy Beef Sandwiches, 18
Easy Beef Stew, 14
Easy Beef Stroganoff, 60
Niku Jaga (Japanese Beef Stew), 214
Russian Borscht, 224
Smothered Steak, 10
So Simple Supper!, 16
Super-Easy Beef Burritos, 60
Sweet and Sour Brisket Stew, 262
Swiss Steak Stew, 18

Beef (continued)

Veggie Soup with Beef, 10

Wild Mushroom Beef Stew, 264

Beef Fajita Soup, 266

Beef, Ground

Chorizo Chili, 36

Easy Chili, 20

Grandma Ruth's Minestrone, 258

Hamburger Soup, 256

Hamburger Veggie Soup, 260

Hearty Meatball Stew, 240

Mexican Cheese Soup, 252

Tavern Burger, 12

Beef Stew with Molasses and Raisins, 268

Beer

Cerveza Chicken Enchilada Casserole, 156

Polska Kielbasa with Beer & Onions, 68

Beggar's Chowder, 250

Best-Ever Roast, 8

Bisque: Celery-Leek Bisque, 210

Bistro Chicken in Rich Cream Sauce, 144

Black and White Chili, 118

Black Bean Chipotle Soup, 222

Braised Italian Chicken with Tomatoes and Olives, 179

Butternut Squash-Apple Soup, 200

C

Cape Cod Stew, 248

Carne Rellenos, 58

Cashew Chicken, 170

Cashews: Cashew Chicken, 170

Cauliflower Soup, 212

Celery-Leek Bisque, 210

Cerveza Chicken Enchilada Casserole, 156

Cheesy Corn and Peppers, 72

Cheesy Slow Cooker Chicken, 51

Cherry Delight, 88

Cherry Rice Pudding, 98

Chicken and Artichoke-Parmesan Dressing, 143

Chicken and Asiago Stuffed Mushrooms, 107

Chicken & Barley Soup, 272

Chicken and Black Bean Chili, 134

Chicken and Chile Pepper Stew, 130

Chicken and Ham with Biscuits, 178

Chicken and Mushroom Fettuccine Alfredo, 188

Chicken & Rice, 162

Chicken and Spicy Black Bean Tacos, 180

Chicken and Sweet Potato Stew, 133

Chicken and Vegetable Chowder, 132

Chicken and Wild Rice Soup, 278

Chicken, Breasts

Asian Chicken "Fondue," 115

Asian Lettuce Wraps, 112

Autumn Chicken, 162

Bistro Chicken in Rich Cream Sauce, 144

Cashew Chicken, 170

Cerveza Chicken Enchilada Casserole, 156

Cheesy Slow Cooker Chicken, 51

Chicken and Artichoke-Parmesan Dressing, 143

Chicken and Mushroom Fettuccine Alfredo, 188

Chicken & Rice, 162

Chicken and Spicy Black Bean Tacos, 180

Chicken and Sweet Potato Stew, 133

Chicken and Vegetable Chowder, 132

Chicken and Wild Rice Soup, 278

Chicken Croustade, 104

Chicken Fiesta Soup, 276

Chicken in Honey Sauce, 164

Chicken, Breasts (continued)

Chicken Parisienne, 169

Chicken Parmesan with Eggplant, 150

Chicken Stew with Herb Dumplings, 125

Chicken Tortilla Soup, 120

Coq au Vin, 148

Creamy Chicken, 40

Creamy Chicken and Mushrooms, 184

Greek Chicken Pitas with Creamy Mustard Sauce, 174

Greek-Style Chicken Stew, 124

Heidi's Chicken Supreme, 52

Herbed Artichoke Chicken, 168

Hot & Sour Chicken, 68

Mediterranean Chicken Breasts and Wild Rice, 158

Quatro Frijoles con Pollo Cantaro, 128

Sandy's Mexican Chicken, 66

Slow Cooker Chicken and Dressing, 44

Slow Cooker Chicken Dinner, 46

Spicy Shredded Chicken, 53

Stuffed Chicken Breasts, 138

Chicken Cacciatore, 186

Chicken Croustade, 104

Chicken Fiesta Soup, 276

Chicken, Ground

Stuffed Baby Bell Peppers, 100

Thai Coconut Chicken Meatballs, 116

Chicken in Honey Sauce, 164

Chicken Liver Pâté, 108

Chicken, Livers: Chicken Liver Pâté, 108

Chicken, Miscellaneous

Chicken and Ham with Biscuits, 178

Mile-High Enchilada Pie, 69

Thai Chicken, 154

Chicken Parisienne, 169
Chicken Parmesan with
    Eggplant, 150
Chicken, Sausage
Chicken and Asiago
    Stuffed Mushrooms, 107
Chicken Sausage Pilaf, 50
Chicken Sausage Pilaf, 50
Chicken Stew with Herb
    Dumplings, 125
Chicken Tangier, 136
Chicken, Tenders
Black and White Chili, 118
Chicken Cacciatore, 186
Chicken Teriyaki, 164
Country Chicken
    Chowder, 274
Chicken Teriyaki, 164
Chicken, Thighs
Asian Barbecue Skewers,
    102
Braised Italian Chicken
    with Tomatoes and
    Olives, 179
Chicken and Black Bean
    Chili, 134
Chicken and Chile Pepper
    Stew, 130
Chicken Tangier, 136
Chinese Chicken Stew,
    122
Chipotle Chicken
    Casserole, 161
Chipotle Chicken Stew,
    126
Creamy Farmhouse
    Chicken and Garden
    Soup, 280
Curry Chicken with
    Mango and Red
    Pepper, 182
Dijon Chicken Thighs with
    Artichoke Sauce, 160
Easy Cheesy Aruban-
    Inspired Chicken, 142
Greek Chicken and Orzo,
    151
Indian-Style Apricot
    Chicken, 146
Provençal Lemon and
    Olive Chicken, 166
Spanish Paella with
    Chicken and Sausage,
    172

Chicken, Thighs
(continued)
Tender Asian-Style
    Chicken, 185
Traditional Cassoulet,
    190
Chicken Tortilla Soup, 120
Chicken, Whole
Basque Chicken with
    Peppers, 152
Chicken & Barley Soup,
    272
Forty-Clove Chicken, 140
Hearty Chicken Tequila
    Soup, 270
Roast Chicken with Peas,
    Prosciutto and Cream,
    176
Chicken, Wings
Angel Wings, 106
Cranberry-Barbecue
    Chicken Wings, 114
Honey-Glazed Chicken
    Wings, 106
Moroccan Spiced Chicken
    Wings, 110
Oriental Chicken Wings,
    110
Chilies
Black and White Chili,
    118
Chicken and Black Bean
    Chili, 134
Chorizo Chili, 36
Easy Chili, 20
Chili Verde, 54
Chinese Chicken Stew, 122
Chipotle Chicken Casserole,
    161
Chipotle Chicken Stew,
    126
Chorizo Chili, 36
Chowders
Beggar's Chowder, 250
Chicken and Vegetable
    Chowder, 132
Country Chicken
    Chowder, 274
Double Corn Chowder,
    194
Manhattan Clam
    Chowder, 202
Navy Bean Bacon
    Chowder, 246

Cinnamon-Ginger Poached
    Pears, 90
Cinn-Sational Swirl Cake, 86
Citrus Chinese Dates with
    Toasted Hazelnuts, 96
Clams: Manhattan Clam
    Chowder, 202
Classic French Onion Soup,
    198
Cod: Cape Cod Stew, 248
Coq au Vin, 148
Corned Beef and Cabbage,
    56
Country Chicken Chowder,
    274
Country-Style Steak, 16
Cranberry-Barbecue
    Chicken Wings, 114
Creamy Chicken, 40
Creamy Chicken and
    Mushrooms, 184
Creamy Farmhouse Chicken
    and Garden Soup, 280
Curried Sweet Potato and
    Carrot Soup, 192
Curry Chicken with Mango
    and Red Pepper, 182

D
Dad's Dill Beef Roast, 12
Dijon Chicken Thighs with
    Artichoke Sauce, 160
Double Corn Chowder, 194

E
Easy Beef Sandwiches, 18
Easy Beef Stew, 14
Easy Beef Stroganoff, 60
Easy Cheesy Aruban-
    Inspired Chicken, 142
Easy Chili, 20
Easy Chocolate Pudding
    Cake, 84
Easy Dirty Rice, 74
Easy Homemade Barbecue
    Sandwiches, 34
Easy Pork Chop Dinner, 32

F
Forty-Clove Chicken, 140
French Lentil Rice Soup, 220
French Onion Soup, 22
Fresh Lime and Black Bean
    Soup, 232

G

Garden Potato Casserole, 80
Grandma Ruth's Minestrone, 258
Granny's Apple Cidered Onion Soup with Gouda Cinnamon Toast, 208
Greek Chicken and Orzo, 151
Greek Chicken Pitas with Creamy Mustard Sauce, 174
Greek Lemon and Rice Soup, 228
Greek-Style Chicken Stew, 124

H

Hamburger Soup, 256
Hamburger Veggie Soup, 260
Ham, Proscuitto and Canadian Bacon
Basque Chicken with Peppers, 152
Chicken and Ham with Biscuits, 178
Double Corn Chowder, 194
Old-Fashioned Split Pea Soup, 38
Roast Chicken with Peas, Prosciutto and Cream, 176
Scalloped Potatoes & Ham, 30
Tuscany Bean and Prosciutto Soup, 226
Hazelnuts: Citrus Chinese Dates with Toasted Hazelnuts, 96
Hearty Chicken Tequila Soup, 270
Hearty Lentil and Root Vegetable Stew, 236
Hearty Meatball Stew, 240
Hearty Mushroom and Barley Soup, 234
Heidi's Chicken Supreme, 52
Herbed Artichoke Chicken, 168
Herbed Turkey Breast with Orange Sauce, 48
Hominy: Double Corn Chowder, 194

Honey-Glazed Chicken Wings, 106
Hot & Sour Chicken, 68

I

Indian-Style Apricot Chicken, 146
Italian Hillside Garden Soup, 230

L

Lentils
French Lentil Rice Soup, 220
Hearty Lentil and Root Vegetable Stew, 236
Linguiça & Green Bean Soup, 238

M

Mango Ginger Pork Roast, 64
Manhattan Clam Chowder, 202
Mediterranean Chicken Breasts and Wild Rice, 158
Mediterranean Shrimp Soup, 216
Mexican Cheese Soup, 252
Mile-High Enchilada Pie, 69
Minestrone alla Milanese, 218
Moroccan Spiced Chicken Wings, 110
Mushrooms
Asian Beef Stew, 254
Asian Chicken "Fondue," 115
Asian Lettuce Wraps, 112
Autumn Chicken, 162
Basque Chicken with Peppers, 152
Beggar's Chowder, 250
Cashew Chicken, 170
Chicken and Asiago Stuffed Mushrooms, 107
Chicken and Mushroom Fettuccine Alfredo, 188
Chicken and Vegetable Chowder, 132
Chicken Cacciatore, 186
Chicken Croustade, 104
Chicken Parisienne, 169
Chicken Stew with Herb Dumplings, 125

Mushrooms (continued)
Chinese Chicken Stew, 122
Coq au Vin, 148
Creamy Chicken, 40
Creamy Chicken and Mushrooms, 184
Dijon Chicken Thighs with Artichoke Sauce, 160
Easy Beef Stew, 14
Greek-Style Chicken Stew, 124
Hearty Mushroom and Barley Soup, 234
Mediterranean Shrimp Soup, 216
Wild Mushroom Beef Stew, 264
Mussels: Cape Cod Stew, 248
My Mother's Sausage and Vegetable Soup, 242

N

Navy Bean Bacon Chowder, 246
Niku Jaga (Japanese Beef Stew), 214
Nuts (see also **Almonds; Cashews; Hazelnuts; Peanuts; Pecans; Pine Nuts; Walnuts):** Streusel Pound Cake, 94

O

Old-Fashioned Split Pea Soup, 38
Orange-Spice Glazed Carrots, 83
Oriental Chicken Wings, 112

P

Parmesan Potato Wedges, 76
Pasta
Chicken and Mushroom Fettuccine Alfredo, 188
Chicken Parisienne, 169
Chicken Sausage Pilaf, 50
Creamy Farmhouse Chicken and Garden Soup, 280
Grandma Ruth's Minestrone, 258
Greek Chicken and Orzo, 151

Pasta (continued)
  Greek-Style Chicken Stew, 124
  Hamburger Soup, 256
  Italian Hillside Garden Soup, 230
  Penne Pasta Zuppa, 196
  Rich and Hearty Drumstick Soup, 244
  Roast Chicken with Peas, Prosciutto and Cream, 176
"Peachy Keen" Dessert Treat, 88
Peanuts: Thai Chicken, 154
Pecans: Triple Chocolate Fantasy, 92
Penne Pasta Zuppa, 196
Pesto Rice and Beans, 78
Pine Nuts: Barley with Currants and Pine Nuts, 70
Polska Kielbasa with Beer & Onions, 68
Pork (see also **Bacon; Ham, Proscuitto and Candian Bacon; Sausage**)
  Chili Verde, 54
  Easy Pork Chop Dinner, 32
  Mango Ginger Pork Roast, 64
  Shredded Pork Wraps, 26
  Simply Delicious Pork, 36
  Slow-Cooked Pork & Sauerkraut, 32
  Steamed Pork Buns, 28
Potato Cheddar Soup, 204
Potatoes (see also **Potatoes, Sweet**)
  Best-Ever Roast, 8
  Chicken and Chile Pepper Stew, 130
  Chicken and Sweet Potato Stew, 133
  Chicken Stew with Herb Dumplings, 125
  Easy Pork Chop Dinner, 32
  Garden Potato Casserole, 80
  Manhattan Clam Chowder, 202

Potatoes (continued)
  Minestrone alla Milanese, 218
  My Mother's Sausage and Vegetable Soup, 242
  Niku Jaga (Japanese Beef Stew), 214
  Parmesan Potato Wedges, 76
  Penne Pasta Zuppa, 196
  Potato Cheddar Soup, 204
  Rustic Garlic Mashed Potatoes, 76
  Scalloped Potatoes & Ham, 30
  Vegetable Medley Soup, 206
  Wild Mushroom Beef Stew, 264
Potatoes, Sweet
  Chicken and Sweet Potato Stew, 133
  Curried Sweet Potato and Carrot Soup, 192
  Sweet-Spiced Sweet Potatoes, 82
  Vegetable Medley Soup, 206
Provençal Lemon and Olive Chicken, 166
Pumpkin-Cranberry Custard, 90

Q
Quatro Frijoles con Pollo Cantaro, 128

R
Rice
  Cherry Rice Pudding, 98
  Chicken & Rice, 162
  Chicken and Wild Rice Soup, 278
  Chicken Sausage Pilaf, 50
  Chicken Teriyaki, 164
  Easy Dirty Rice, 74
  French Lentil Rice Soup, 220
  Greek Lemon and Rice Soup, 228
  Mediterranean Chicken Breasts and Wild Rice, 158

Rice (continued)
  Pesto Rice and Beans, 78
  Spanish Paella with Chicken and Sausage, 172
  Stuffed Baby Bell Peppers, 100
  Rich and Hearty Drumstick Soup, 244
  Roast Chicken with Peas, Prosciutto and Cream, 176
  Russian Borscht, 224
  Rustic Garlic Mashed Potatoes, 76

S
Sandy's Mexican Chicken, 66
Sausage
  Chorizo Chili, 36
  Easy Dirty Rice, 74
  Linguiça & Green Bean Soup, 238
  Polska Kielbasa with Beer & Onions, 68
  Spanish Paella with Chicken and Sausage, 172
  Traditional Cassoulet, 190
Scalloped Potatoes & Ham, 30
Shredded Pork Wraps, 26
Shrimp
  Asian Lettuce Wraps, 112
  Cape Cod Stew, 248
  Mediterranean Shrimp Soup, 216
Simply Delicious Pork, 36
Slow-Cooked Pork & Sauerkraut, 32
Slow Cooker Chicken and Dressing, 44
Slow Cooker Chicken Dinner, 46
Smothered Steak, 10
So Simple Supper!, 16
Soups
  Beef Fajita Soup, 266
  Black Bean Chipotle Soup, 222
  Butternut Squash-Apple Soup, 200
  Cauliflower Soup, 212

Soups (continued)
Chicken and Wild Rice Soup, 278
Chicken Fiesta Soup, 276
Chicken Tortilla Soup, 120
Classic French Onion Soup, 198
Creamy Farmhouse Chicken and Garden Soup, 280
Curried Sweet Potato and Carrot Soup, 192
French Lentil Rice Soup, 220
French Onion Soup, 22
Fresh Lime and Black Bean Soup, 232
Granny's Apple Cidered Onion Soup with Gouda Cinnamon Toast, 208
Greek Lemon and Rice Soup, 228
Hamburger Soup, 256
Hearty Chicken Tequila Soup, 270
Hearty Mushroom and Barley Soup, 234
Italian Hillside Garden Soup, 230
Linguiça & Green Bean Soup, 238
Mediterranean Shrimp Soup, 216
Mexican Cheese Soup, 252
My Mother's Sausage and Vegetable Soup, 242
Old-Fashioned Split Pea Soup, 38
Potato Cheddar Soup, 204
Rich and Hearty Drumstick Soup, 244
Tuscany Bean and Prosciutto Soup, 226
Vegetable Medley Soup, 206
Veggie Soup with Beef, 10
Spanish Paella with Chicken and Sausage, 172
Spicy Shredded Chicken, 53
Spicy Turkey with Citrus au Jus, 42

Spinach Gorgonzola Cornbread, 82
Steamed Pork Buns, 28
Stews
Asian Beef Stew, 254
Beef Stew with Molasses and Raisins, 268
Cape Cod Stew, 248
Chicken and Chile Pepper Stew, 130
Chicken and Sweet Potato Stew, 133
Chicken Stew with Herb Dumplings, 125
Chinese Chicken Stew, 122
Chipotle Chicken Stew, 126
Easy Beef Stew, 14
Greek-Style Chicken Stew, 124
Hearty Lentil and Root Vegetable Stew, 236
Hearty Meatball Stew, 240
Niku Jaga (Japanese Beef Stew), 214
Sweet and Sour Brisket Stew, 262
Swiss Steak Stew, 18
Wild Mushroom Beef Stew, 264
Streusel Pound Cake, 94
Stuffed Baby Bell Peppers, 100
Stuffed Chicken Breasts, 138
Super-Easy Beef Burritos, 60
Sweet and Sour Brisket Stew, 262
Sweet-Spiced Sweet Potatoes, 82
Swiss Steak Stew, 18

T

Tavern Burger, 12
Tender Asian-Style Chicken, 185
Thai Chicken, 154
Thai Coconut Chicken Meatballs, 116
Traditional Cassoulet, 190
Triple Chocolate Fantasy, 92

Turkey, Breasts
Herbed Turkey Breast with Orange Sauce, 48
Spicy Turkey with Citrus au Jus, 42
Turkey, Drumsticks or Legs
Beggar's Chowder, 250
Rich and Hearty Drumstick Soup, 244
Turkey, Sausage: My Mother's Sausage and Vegetable Soup, 242
Tuscany Bean and Prosciutto Soup, 226

V

Vegetable Medley Soup, 206
Veggie Soup with Beef, 10

W

Walnuts: Cherry Delight, 88
Wild Mushroom Beef Stew, 264
Wine
Autumn Chicken, 162
Basque Chicken with Peppers, 152
Bistro Chicken in Rich Cream Sauce, 144
Braised Italian Chicken with Tomatoes and Olives, 179
Chicken and Asiago Stuffed Mushrooms, 107
Chicken Croustade, 104
Chicken Parisienne, 169
Chicken Tangier, 136
Classic French Onion Soup, 198
Coq au Vin, 148
Creamy Chicken and Mushrooms, 184
Easy Beef Stew, 14
Forty-Clove Chicken, 140
Herbed Artichoke Chicken, 168
Niku Jaga (Japanese Beef Stew), 214
Oriental Chicken Wings, 110
Roast Chicken with Peas, Prosciutto and Cream, 176
Traditional Cassoulet, 190

METRIC CONVERSION CHART

VOLUME MEASUREMENTS (dry)

1/8 teaspoon = 0.5 mL
1/4 teaspoon = 1 mL
1/2 teaspoon = 2 mL
3/4 teaspoon = 4 mL
1 teaspoon = 5 mL
1 tablespoon = 15 mL
2 tablespoons = 30 mL
1/4 cup = 60 mL
1/3 cup = 75 mL
1/2 cup = 125 mL
2/3 cup = 150 mL
3/4 cup = 175 mL
1 cup = 250 mL
2 cups = 1 pint = 500 mL
3 cups = 750 mL
4 cups = 1 quart = 1 L

VOLUME MEASUREMENTS (fluid)

1 fluid ounce (2 tablespoons) = 30 mL
4 fluid ounces (1/2 cup) = 125 mL
8 fluid ounces (1 cup) = 250 mL
12 fluid ounces (1 1/2 cups) = 375 mL
16 fluid ounces (2 cups) = 500 mL

WEIGHTS (mass)

1/2 ounce = 15 g
1 ounce = 30 g
3 ounces = 90 g
4 ounces = 120 g
8 ounces = 225 g
10 ounces = 285 g
12 ounces = 360 g
16 ounces = 1 pound = 450 g

DIMENSIONS

1/16 inch = 2 mm
1/8 inch = 3 mm
1/4 inch = 6 mm
1/2 inch = 1.5 cm
3/4 inch = 2 cm
1 inch = 2.5 cm

OVEN TEMPERATURES

250°F = 120°C
275°F = 140°C
300°F = 150°C
325°F = 160°C
350°F = 180°C
375°F = 190°C
400°F = 200°C
425°F = 220°C
450°F = 230°C

BAKING PAN AND DISH EQUIVALENTS

Utensil	Size in Inches	Size in Centimeters	Volume	Metric Volume
Baking or Cake Pan (square or rectangular)	8×8×2	20×20×5	8 cups	2 L
	9×9×2	23×23×5	10 cups	2.5 L
	13×9×2	33×23×5	12 cups	3 L
Loaf Pan	8½×4½×2½	21×11×6	6 cups	1.5 L
	9×9×3	23×13×7	8 cups	2 L
Round Layer Cake Pan	8×1½	20×4	4 cups	1 L
	9×1½	23×4	5 cups	1.25 L
Pie Plate	8×1½	20×4	4 cups	1 L
	9×1½	23×4	5 cups	1.25 L
Baking Dish or Casserole			1 quart/4 cups	1 L
			1½ quart/6 cups	1.5 L
			2 quart/8 cups	2 L
			3 quart/12 cups	3 L